word alive

-depth Small Group
ble Studies

EADER'S
GUIDE

Daniel

DANIEL

daring faith in dangerous times

Case Van Kempen

FAITH
ALIVE®
Christian Resources

Grand Rapids, Michigan

Cover photo: Taxi

Faith Alive Christian Resources published by CRC Publications.
Word Alive: In-depth Small Group Bible Studies
Daniel: Daring Faith in Dangerous Times (Leader's Guide), © 2003 by CRC
Publications, 2850 Kalamazoo Ave. SE, Grand Rapids, MI 49560. All rights
reserved. With the exception of brief excerpts for review purposes, no part of
this book may be reproduced in any manner whatsoever without written
permission from the publisher. Printed in the United States of America on
recycled paper.

We welcome your comments. Call us at 1-800-333-8300 or e-mail us at
editors@FaithAliveResources.org.

ISBN 1-56212-983-X

10 9 8 7 6 5 4 3 2 1

Contents

Introduction

This *Word Alive* leader's guide provides background information and discussion suggestions for the in-depth small group adult Bible study *Daniel: Daring Faith in Dangerous Times.* Case Van Kempen, author of this leader's guide and the accompanying study guide, is a minister in the Reformed Church in America. He has served churches in Clymer, New York; Franklin Lakes, New Jersey; and Holland, Michigan. He and his wife, Leigh, currently live in Holland, and they have three children: Abigail, Peter, and Paul. Case is also the author of *Hard Questions People Ask About the Christian Faith* (Faith Alive, 2002).

Each member of your group, including each leader, should have a study guide to use during this Bible study.

Using This Leader's Guide

This leader's guide is intended to be only what its title conveys: a guide. It is not meant to be followed like a cookbook, step by step. It offers suggestions rather than prescriptions. As a discussion leader, you should adapt all materials and procedures in this leader's guide to suit the needs and abilities of your group members.

For each lesson in the accompanying study guide, this leader's guide adds background and supplementary material that you, as leader, can share as you see fit to enhance your group's discussion of the lesson. This guide also includes answers to the General Discussion questions posed in the study guide. These answers are meant to provide you with a beginning point for discussion, if you find that useful. No claim is made for completeness, however, or for having the "last word."

You'll also notice a brief lesson plan for small group use (explained below) in both the study guide and this leader's guide. We hope you find this feature useful as you and your group explore this in-depth Bible study together.

Use what you can in this leader's guide, but feel free to adapt, substitute, and revise. Pose your own questions and seek answers based on your study and on the insights of group members. Your ultimate goal is not simply to cover the lesson material but to lead the group into an encounter with the living Word of God.

Small Group Study

Each of the following lessons contains a basic lesson plan that you can use or adapt to suit your own small group's style and needs. You'll find the lesson plan under Small Group Session Ideas at the end of each lesson's material in both the study guide and this leader's guide.

Small groups tend to use various kinds of formats in their meetings. Some groups meet for a couple of hours every week; others meet for an hour every two or three weeks. Some study the Bible for an hour and then divide into groups of two or three for an additional hour of confidential prayer-and-share time; others study the Bible for a half to three-quarters of an hour and then spend about fifteen minutes in sharing and prayer. The formats may vary from one small group strategy to the next, but each one will usually include most of the elements found in the basic plan suggested in this study series. So whatever format you're used to, we hope you'll find most of the elements in the lesson plan adaptable to your group and to its particular style and needs. Feel free to add, omit, reorganize, or change any of the elements you find in this basic plan.

The lesson plan includes the essential elements of a small group study, so if you're new to the small group approach and you'd like to try it, this will give you a taste of what small group study is like. Many groups that have tried the small group approach find it extremely rewarding, mainly because the elements of sharing one's feelings and giving one's personal input can become trust-building and friendship-building and confidence-building when coupled with group confidentiality and integrity. Within the body of Christ and with direction provided by the Word of God, small group study can result in fellowship and spiritual growth, to God's glory. While being inwardly focused in the areas of sharing and developing personal expression, the small group approach, if it's healthy, also focuses on looking and reaching outward for the benefit of others. Both the inward and the outward focuses are essential in the church and in the individual Christian life.

Here's a brief overview of the basic plan you'll find under Small Group Session Ideas in each lesson:

• The lesson plan is divided into several timed sections to help you keep pace for your group's meeting time. The suggested times for each section total about 60-75 minutes. Some groups will use 75 minutes or more; others will use 60 minutes or even less. Use whatever time your group needs or is most comfortable with. Never feel pressured to work through all of the discussion questions if you don't have enough time. Pick and choose the ones you and your group think are appropriate or most applicable.

- For the *Opening* of your session we suggest a brief time for beginning with prayer and with sharing your past week's experiences, especially with regard to any personal and spiritual goals you've set. You may also wish to include singing or a devotional reading during this time. Then we invite you to focus on main points of the lesson to keep in mind as you move into Bible study.

- The *Growing* section of your session includes some brief suggestions on reading the Scripture passage and the study guide notes, if your group likes to read before getting into discussion. *Group members should be aware that it's important to at least read through the Scripture and study guide notes before meeting together. They may also wish to prepare answers to discussion questions before meeting.* Also included are suggestions for using some of the General Discussion questions along with process questions that are designed specifically for small group use. These questions generally guide your thinking process from *what you think* to *what you might do in Jesus' name* in view of the topic for a particular session.

- The next section is *Goalsetting,* in which you commit to a personal spiritual goal as a result of the Bible study you have just completed.

- The *Closing* section of your session includes a time for sharing prayer concerns and praises before you join with the group in a concluding prayer.

- Several sessions also include group project ideas that some or all of your group members may wish to try. The projects are for study or hands-on work or both, and their purpose is for outreach or for teaching that can enhance the group's outward focus.

Using the Study Guide

Each person in your group should have a study guide to use at home and during meetings. The material for each lesson in the study guide includes the Scripture passage to be studied, thought-provoking notes and commentary on the Scripture, and several discussion questions that will help your group apply the Scripture to their daily living.

Some groups like to read the Scripture passage and the lesson notes during their meeting—and that can be helpful for making the material fresh in everyone's mind while doing the session together. Because of the volume of material in each lesson, however, we suggest that group members spend twenty minutes or so familiarizing themselves with the lesson material ahead of time so that when everyone meets together, any reading will serve as review and the group can move efficiently into discussion time.

Your Role as Leader

Being a leader of adults can be a serious, humbling business. While you're preparing for a lesson, the doubts may come thick and fast: "How did I get talked into this? I'm no Bible scholar . . . no teacher. . . . How do I dare instruct my friends from church in the Word of God?" If that happens, be reminded that leading a group is more than methodology, more than a grab bag of skills. Leading a group study is a calling for which God's Spirit will equip you.

And leading a group is not the same as teaching. A teacher is somewhat of an "authority" on his or her subject; a leader is less so. A teacher may be somewhat separated from the class; a leader is part of the group. A teacher carefully works toward specific objectives, often centered on mastery of content; a group leader works more with process and people than with objectives, seeking to encourage each person to participate and grow. Together, leader and group seek to understand and obey the Word of God. Together they share their questions and insights. Together they pray for one another and strengthen one another.

When you meet with your group, Christ will be there by your side, through his Word and Spirit, gathering his people. This is what makes your role possible . . . and profitable.

Our prayers go with you as you lead others.

—Faith Alive Christian Resources

1

DANIEL 1:1-21

Strangers in a Strange Land

In a Nutshell

Our introduction to the story of Daniel and his companions begins with a brief history of the time in which they lived. As we learn how they came to be exiled from their homes in Judah and underwent training to serve the king of Babylon, we can see how God faithfully provided for them to be obedient to the true King of their lives.

Why Bother Studying Daniel?

Although the circumstances of Daniel's life in Babylon—palace intrigue, inscrutable dreams, disembodied handwriting, and even a cud-chewing king—seem as far-removed and foreign to us as we can imagine, the prophet's responses to every situation teach us valuable lessons in faith. Not only Daniel but also his three companions give vivid testimony to the power of trust and obedience as they try to live faithfully for God in dangerous times. These virtues are as necessary today as in any other period in history, and Daniel is an excellent tutor in helping us decide how to live by faith in a rapidly changing world. In case any group members are wondering whether this study is worth their time, you may want to open (in connection with General Discussion question 1) with some honest discussion on that very topic, asking questions like these:

- Why should we bother studying Daniel?
- How can this book be relevant to our lives?
- What expectations can we or should we have as we get into this study?

Encourage everyone to listen open-mindedly to each other, and note some of the positive comments mentioned here along with other good reasons for Bible study. For a few words from the Bible itself, you may wish to read together and reflect on the following brief passages: Deuteronomy 6:4-7; Psalm 119:105; 2 Timothy 3:16-17.

Trust and Obey

In this lesson we begin our study of Daniel's life by reviewing the history of Judah's final years. As we consider how Daniel and his friends came to be in Babylon, it might be easy to get bogged down in historical details. These are important, of course, but for the opening lesson of this study it may be sufficient simply to emphasize that Daniel and his friends ended up in Babylon because Judah's leaders failed to trust and obey God. When they turned to their neighbors for help instead of trusting in God's protection, their almost-complete lack of obedience resulted in sieges and invasions that ultimately destroyed their nation.

Consider together what God had said years earlier through the prophet Isaiah about forming alliances with other nations:

> "Woe to the obstinate children,"
>> declares the LORD,
> "to those who carry out plans that are not mine,
>> forming an alliance, but not by my Spirit,
>> heaping sin upon sin;
> who go down to Egypt
>> without consulting me;
> who look for help to Pharaoh's protection,
>> to Egypt's shade for refuge."   (Isa. 30:1-2)

The final kings who served in Judah had not only neglected God's warnings through the prophets but also had clearly forgotten the words of King David in Psalm 20:7: "Some trust in chariots and some in horses, but we trust in the name of the LORD our God." If the last kings of Judah had listened to the Lord and his servants, Daniel and his companions might never have gone into Babylonian exile.

Jerusalem's Last Days

Some members of your group may be wondering what happened in Judah after Daniel and his friends were taken to Babylon. We can piece together some details from 2 Kings 24-25 and 2 Chronicles 36. For a more in-depth account, you may wish to study the life of Jeremiah, one of the last prophets of Judah before the fall of Jerusalem (see especially Jer. 1; 7; 19-20; 36-40; 52).

Back in Judah, while King Jehoiakim and others, including Daniel, journeyed off to exile in Babylon (2 Chron. 36:6; Dan. 1:2, 6), eighteen-year-old Jehoiachin of Judah succeeded his father as king (2 Kings 24:8). Jehoiachin also committed evil in God's sight, and his rule lasted only three months, like that of his uncle Jehoahaz. During his brief reign the second Babylonian invasion took place (597 B.C.), resulting in even more Judean people being taken away to Babylon—including Jehoiachin (24:12-16).

Nebuchadnezzar then made Jehoiachin's uncle Mattaniah (meaning "gift of Yahweh") the new vassal-king, changing his name to Zedekiah ("righteousness of Yahweh"). Zedekiah also did evil in the sight of the Lord (would this family never learn?), and after nine years he attempted a final rebellion against Babylon. In response, Babylon laid siege to Jerusalem for nearly two years while fighting other battles elsewhere. Second Kings 25 vividly describes Jerusalem's last days in the eleventh year of Zedekiah's reign—no food, no security, no place to hide. The final destruction was so swift, vicious, and thorough that by 586 B.C. Nebuchadnezzar no longer had to worry about rebellion from the people of Judah, for Judah had ceased to exist.

New Kids on the Block

After the first few sentences, the opening scenes of Daniel shift quickly from Judah to the capital of the new world power, Babylon. Living as we do in a land where a fast-food restaurant on one coast serves the same menu as a fast-food restaurant on the opposite coast, it can be easy to overlook that a journey of less than a thousand miles brought Daniel and his companions into an utterly foreign culture.

Arriving in Babylon, they might have first noticed the strange architecture, including the *ziggurat*, a kind of terraced pyramid (Gen. 11). They would soon have been introduced to the temples of the local deities, including Bel, Marduk, and Ea, the supreme triad (although there were hundreds of other, lesser deities in the pantheon) of Babylonian gods. The youths from Judah would also have observed strange clothing, strange customs, and, not insignificantly, strange food.

Ashpenaz, Nebuchadnezzar's chief of staff, was charged with training these young captives in the language and literature of Babylon. Apparently it was important to the king to have palace servants who were not only "handsome" and "without any physical defect" but also well versed in the customs and practices of their new home (Dan. 1:4).

As noted in the study guide, the Babylonian language was no doubt a challenge to learn, utilizing an alphabet with hundreds of symbols (see Additional Notes on Dan. 1:4). The literature must also have been daunting, for the tales and legends of the Babylonians and their ancestors trace back to before 2800 B.C. In the course of their studies, Daniel and his friends may well have come across stories about the legendary Babylonian king, Gilgamesh, whose saga (*The Epic of Gilgamesh*, c. 2000 B.C.) contains a flood story similar to that of the flood account in Genesis 6-8. They may also have taken an interest in reading about "Ur of the Chaldeans," Abraham's ancestral home (Gen. 11:31). Ur was located about 100 miles downriver from Babylon along the Euphrates (toward the Persian Gulf), and in Daniel's day it was still an important city in the empire.

GENERAL DISCUSSION

1. *Why do you think God's Word contains so many passages that can best be described as history? Do you think people in general, and people who attend church in particular, are well versed in the history of God's people, both before and after the time of Jesus? What value is there in making the effort to learn more about this history?*

Depending on how well you know your study group (you certainly don't want to embarrass anyone), you may want to try this simple exercise: Hand out a list of the names of several well-known biblical figures—for example, Moses, Matthew, Abraham, Paul, Sarah, David, Peter, Esther, Daniel, and Jacob—and ask each person to place the figures in chronological order. Unless you're leading an exceptional group, you'll probably find that only a few are able to do this exercise accurately. (Even these few may give you a puzzled expression if you ask them to also give an approximate date for each character.) As familiar as we are with many individual stories in God's Word, we often tend to focus on them separately rather than seeing how they all connect in the broad sweep of biblical history.

The Bible itself doesn't help much with an exercise like this, of course, since its sixty-six books are not arranged in a tidy, chronological sequence. (In some books even the chapters are not arranged chronologically! For example, see

Jeremiah.) Several of the historical books overlap, covering the same period of time. The books of the prophets, though placed near the end of the Old Testament, fit into various time periods covered in the earlier-placed historical books. And then there's the book of Job, which seems to defy any kind of accurate dating.

In light of this chronological confusion, it may be worth spending a little time setting Daniel in its historical context. Many Bible dictionaries and study Bibles provide time lines that can help us learn when Daniel lived (around 620-535 B.C.) and how the events in his book of prophecy fit into God's salvation history.

Once you've established Daniel's time period, you can begin to share answers about why it's important to know about the history of the Bible. Someone may start off with a version of the well-known saying "Those who cannot remember the past are condemned to repeat it" (George Santayana, Spanish-born American philosopher and poet, 1863-1952). And that's not a bad place to begin. Nearly every mistake, folly, blunder, and sin known to humanity can be found somewhere in God's Word, so why should we repeat them? Doesn't it make sense for us to learn from our ancestors' mistakes? Along with these questions, you may want to ask everyone to reflect on biblical or nonbiblical figures who did not remember the past. What were the consequences of their actions?

Someone may also comment that the power of stories—especially true stories from history—tends to shape our thinking. This is a helpful observation; consider how our attitudes in North America have changed on a wide variety of subjects since the terrorist attacks of September 11, 2001. Even though only a few of us have had a close personal connection to those events, the stories surrounding that day will affect the attitudes of everyone who hears them for generations.

Having said all this about the value of learning from our past, there's still the plain fact that history is a subject that fails to generate much excitement. When Hollywood announces the upcoming release of a new science-fiction epic, people line up halfway around the block for the first showing. But when a historical epic hits the screen, you don't have to skip your stop at the concession stand to find a good seat.

Still, in many ways history can be one of our greatest teachers, if we give it the chance. Through the prophet

Isaiah, God commanded, "Remember the former things, those of long ago; I am God, and there is no other; I am God, and there is none like me" (Isa. 46:9). Do we need any other reason to study the history recorded in God's Word?

2. *Nebuchadnezzar laid siege to Jerusalem, finally destroying it in about 586 B.C. What are some ways in which people of faith are under siege from God's enemies today? Do we ever form allegiances with earthly powers instead of placing our trust in God? Explain.*

I work out at a health club that has five TV sets, all tuned to different stations, mounted on a wall near the lineup of treadmill machines. Each morning I stare at the silent images (I don't bother with headphones) and play a little game: *How long will it take before every station shows an image of someone in either their bathing suit or their underwear?* On most days, it doesn't take more than a few minutes (even on the news channels!).

Obviously the simple appearance of someone who is minimally clothed isn't necessarily an immoral display, but the frequency with which such people are shown on TV is just one example of how we are under siege from sexual imagery. In the same way, the media surround us with violence, profanity, moral corruption, and every other kind of biblically proscribed behavior. Perhaps the most pernicious images of all are those that depict material prosperity. Monetary wealth is routinely held out as the only way to achieve a full, joyful life—and many Christians accept that as "gospel."

How does the church deal—or fail to deal—with these enemies of faith? Have we made compromises with the secular world instead of placing our trust in God?

Consider this example: Your teenage child wants to go to a movie that's just opened. "Mom, it's only rated PG-13. Can I go to see it? Pleeeease?" What do you say? What do most people say? Based on my experience in teaching high school students, most parents say yes—if their children even bother to ask at all.

What we can observe here is that many Christian parents have made an informal deal with the movie studios: *If producers will police themselves by using a rating system, parents will let their children attend supposedly age-appropriate films— unmonitored.* The uncomfortable truth, though, is that Christian adults should carefully consider whether any film rated PG-13 or R is appropriate, regardless of the age of the viewer. Even many films with ratings for a more general audience often contain elements that should be thoughtfully considered before allowing young children to view them.

Here's a suggestion I've found to be really helpful: *Christian parents should watch films and TV programs with their children—to acknowledge the good, point out the bad, and, most important, think about ways that we as believers can transform the society we live in.* In their own day, Daniel and his companions did not allow Babylonian practices to corrupt them, even as they lived in the midst of that worldly society.

Film and TV are just two areas of compromise that many believers have made rather than trusting the way of God's wisdom about immorality. Didn't Jesus say, "I tell you that anyone who looks at a woman lustfully has already committed adultery" (Matt. 5:28)? We have to admit this is a hard teaching. We make many other compromises in the areas of fashion, finance, education, and reproductive health (consider the fate of unused embryos following *in vitro* fertilization)—to name just a few. We don't generally use the word *allegiance* in connection with these things, but that word accurately describes the relationship we have with many secular practices and institutions. As Christians, though, we know that our sole allegiance should be with God.

3. *Daniel and his companions were forcibly resettled into a new culture, where God chose to use their extraordinary faith as an example for future generations. Can you think of any contemporary examples of people whose lives have been severely disrupted? How can faith sustain us in such circumstances?*

Depending on the age and makeup of your group, there's a pretty good chance that some members—or their recent ancestors—have had the experience of settling in a new land. Discussion may revolve around language differences, finding work and adequate housing, educational differences, and in some cases the longing to go back to one's country of origin. Christian immigrants have often observed that the hand of God and their faith in God are the things that sustained them through their most difficult times.

Another example that may come up in your discussion is the plight of refugees around the globe. People who are familiar with the situation in Israel may mention that many of the Palestinians who were forced from their homes in the late 1940s are still living in refugee camps today. In light of such situations, we might ask, *How can the gospel turn anger and resentment in refugee situations into constructive action and hope for the future?*

On a lighter note, you could also mention the challenges people face when they go off to college, take a new job in a different state or province, or simply spend an extended time working in a foreign country (an increasingly common practice as more companies want workers to have international experience).

In all such situations and more, faith in the one true God can sustain us by being a steady anchor in uncertain waters. Daniel gives us the example of putting faith first—obeying God's laws, praying to God, trusting God for sustenance and protection. You may also wish to cite some other biblical examples of these practices:

- On obedience, consider Joshua at the city of Jericho (Josh. 6). What happened when he followed God's Word precisely?

- On prayer, consider the apostle Paul in Philippi (Acts 16:25-26). As he and his companions prayed and sung hymns, they were released from prison.

- On sustenance, consider the words of Jesus in his Sermon on the Mount (Matt. 6:25-33). Just as God provides for sparrows and lilies, God will certainly provide for us.

By following these kinds of examples when we're away from familiar surroundings, we become a light to others, we demonstrate the wisdom of God, and we show gratitude for God's never-ending mercy and love.

We may even find that the Lord has already put people in place to help us. Just as God caused Ashpenaz, the chief official, to be sympathetic toward Daniel and his companions (Dan. 1:9), we may find that God has already provided people to help us in our adjustment to a new situation.

4. *Daniel and his friends refused the royal food from the king's table. What does this incident teach us about the saying "When in Rome, do as the Romans do?" Can we learn anything about our own eating habits from this story? What's the most important point for us to learn here?*

As we discover later, it does not appear that Daniel was a committed vegetarian (Dan. 10:3). He was, however, a committed Jew, and he knew that the food of the king's table had not been selected or prepared according to Jewish dietary laws (see Lev. 11 for a brief introduction on what was and wasn't permitted).

It would have been easy for Daniel and his companions to say, "Well, we're not in Jerusalem anymore," and to drop any effort to maintain the eating practices they had learned from childhood. What's more, they were prisoners in exile who were being offered deluxe food from the king's table. Who could blame them for enjoying a few treats?

We face similar temptations whenever we're away from our family, our church, our usual circle of friends, or any other setting or routine that helps us remain faithful. For example, a businessperson on a working trip is offered a few too many drinks and says, "When in Rome . . ." A student off to college for the first time gets invited to an off-campus party and thinks, "When in Rome . . ." A new soldier on an overseas assignment has the choice to join in some weekend revelry and reasons, "When in Rome . . ."

The whole point of the book of Daniel is to encourage us to live faithfully no matter where we are or whom we are with. Faith doesn't change because of geography or sociology.

As far as our eating habits are concerned, Daniel's intent was not to point out the dangers of a high-fat or high-sodium diet. The fact that Daniel and his friends appeared healthier than any of the people eating the king's food was first of all a sign of God's providence, not a proof of the healthful benefits of eating only vegetables. Still, there's at least the suggestion here that vegetables may be better for us than too much "royal food." It's a point worth considering.

The most important point, though, is that we are called to live as God's people no matter where we are. And when we trust and obey God, we can depend on God's providence.

SMALL GROUP SESSION IDEAS

Opening (10 minutes)

Try to arrange for people to be comfortably situated with space for their Bible, study guide, and perhaps something to eat or drink. If this study is being used in a large group or class, consider having everyone sit at round tables in small groups.

If this is a new group, allow some time for introductions. You may find that name tags are also helpful during the first few sessions.

After any necessary introductions, invite everyone to read Psalm 137 quietly (have extra Bibles available, if needed) and to spend a few moments in silence reflecting on the emotions expressed by an anonymous psalmist in exile.

Prayer—Move from reflecting on Psalm 137 to expressing gratitude and praise, acknowledging that God is never far from us, no matter what "strange land" we may be in. Also remember people who, like Daniel, are facing new challenges of faith because of changed circumstances.

Share—Take a few minutes to talk together about the emotions *you* experienced as you thought about Psalm 137. Were you surprised by them? Would you expect Daniel to express similar emotions as he wrote about his experiences in Babylon?

Focus—This lesson's dual emphasis is on the circumstances that brought Daniel and his companions to Babylon and their continuing obedience to God while living in exile. Throughout this time of study, be conscious of the many displaced persons around the world. Remember that someone doesn't have to literally move to another country to feel "exiled." Keep in mind also that God can use times of exile to develop extraordinary faith in people who continue to place their trust in the Lord.

Growing (35-40 minutes)

Read—Daniel is a wonderful book to read out loud, lending itself to dramatic emphasis and timely pauses. If anyone in the group has a gift for expressive reading, invite him or her to read Daniel 1 aloud. As a group, you could also read 2 Kings 23:36-24:7, an account of Nebuchadnezzar's first invasion of Judah (around 605 B.C.), during which Daniel and his friends were taken into exile.

Discuss—Use the following questions along with the General Discussion questions to think about how the stories of Daniel can affect our decision making in our daily living.

• Think about the people of the small nation of Judah, some insisting that their leaders must trust in God alone, others encouraging defensive alliances with other nations. Which side of the debate would you have taken? Explain. Can you think of any ways in which our leaders today face similar decisions?

• Have you ever felt "under siege" as you tried to serve God faithfully? How did you respond to the challenges you faced? Could your experience be a lesson for others? Explain.

• How do people typically react to God when their lives are disrupted? What do our reactions to difficult situations say about our faith?

- Daniel and his companions faced a difficult test of obedience when offered the king's bounty in their new land. What would be a comparable challenge for us, and how could Daniel's response inspire us as we serve God?

Goalsetting (5 minutes)
Look for examples of either displaced people or people "under siege" in the coming week. Note these examples or bring articles about them to the next study session. Focus especially on how God can use people of faith in these kinds of situations.

Closing (10 minutes)
Preparing for Prayer—Encourage everyone to share joys and concerns, including items that have come to mind as a result of this study session. It can be upbuilding to mention answered prayers as well.

Prayer—Open your prayer with Psalm 137:4: "How can we sing the songs of the LORD while in a foreign land?" Acknowledge struggles and concerns, giving others an opportunity to join in, and remember together that because we trust in Jesus, all of this life is lived in the "foreign territory" of this world. Even so, we have much to be thankful for, especially the salvation that will bring us to live in God's presence forever. Pray for strength to live each day by faith while under siege by God's (and our) enemies.

Group Study Project (Optional)
Invite anyone who's interested to research one or more of the historical figures mentioned in Daniel: Nebuchadnezzar, Belshazzar, Cyrus, Darius, and so on. Or maybe someone would like to find or create a time line of events before, during, and after the exile and leading up to the time of Christ. Bible dictionaries and study Bibles can be helpful resources for this kind of study.

2

DANIEL 2

Nebuchadnezzar's Colossal Dream

In a Nutshell

When Nebuchadnezzar makes an impossible request, demanding that his advisers tell him what he dreamed, only Daniel is able to tell the king both the dream and its meaning. In this story we are reminded that no mysteries are hidden from God, that even the greatest human empires are like dust in the wind, and that God's kingdom will never end. We also learn that faith in God leads us to God's truth.

The Despot and the Prophet

If Daniel 1 revealed King Nebuchadnezzar as a shrewd military conqueror, Daniel 2 reveals him as a volatile despot. His short temper may have been the result of his sleeplessness; in any case, the king seemed to be possessed of an explosive personality.

The original emphasis in Daniel 2—that is, the emphasis intended for its first audience—was likely on the king's dream, with its forecast of kingdoms to come. But for modern readers, there may be even more to learn from the contrast between the demanding, threatening king, and the faithful, trusting prophet. If ever there was an example of both a wrong and a right way to face a crisis, this is it!

To lead this lesson effectively, you'll want to keep in balance both the relationship between the king and his various counselors, including Daniel, and the substance of the dream itself.

Good Help Is Hard to Find

First, let's look at the king's relationships. It's hard to imagine why Nebuchadnezzar would have kept his cadre of wise men and advisers around if he suspected they were either (1) incompetent or (2) deceitful, only telling him what he wanted to hear. It might be fun to ask your group if this ever happens today—do presidents, prime ministers, and other national leaders surround themselves with people who tell them only what they want to hear? Or do they seek out people who will tell the truth? Is the same true for corporate executives? What traits do you prefer in a leader?

Someone in the group may observe that the king seemed to enjoy being surrounded by quacks—magicians, enchanters, sorcerers, and the like. It should be noted that these people were not the complete fools they may seem to be from our perspective. The magicians did have a few tricks up their sleeves to impress the people or to frighten the king's enemies (recall the Egyptian magicians who turned rods to snakes or water to blood in the time of Moses—Ex. 7:11, 22). In the same way, the sorcerers most likely were able to read signs from nature and could concoct potions that had some narcotic effects. Astrologers could read the night sky and make learned predictions about the changing of the seasons.

Accurately telling someone what they had dreamed, though, was beyond the ability of any of the usual ancient advisers (it still eludes scientists today!), and the king seemed to suspect that even their dream interpretations might be self-serving. So he came up with a clever twist. Not only would they have to tell him the interpretation of his dream, but they would also have to tell the dream itself. This is something we've never encountered before in any of the dream stories in the Bible.

As the study guide points out, the advisers chose to play dumb, acting as if they hadn't understood what the king wanted. But the king would have none of that. When it was clear they couldn't tell him his dream, he ordered them all killed.

It may seem curious that there was apparently some delay in carrying out the execution order. Nothing in the text suggests that the advisers who were present with the king were instantly slain; in fact, there seems to be pretty good evidence that *no one* was actually put to death following the king's order (Dan. 2:24). While we might expect instant execution, based on our limited knowledge of ancient despots, it may well be that things were done differently in Nebuchadnezzar's Babylon. Notice, for example, that "the decree was issued to put the wise men to death" (2:13); it could take some time for the official decree to be written and dispersed, and it could likewise take a while to search out "all the wise men" of such a large city (and its surrounding towns?) for execution.

At any rate, as soon as the execution order is given, the wise men of Babylon cease to be part of the story. In terms of literary function, they've served their purpose by declaring the impossibility of telling the king his dream. Immediately the narrator cuts to the next scene, in which Daniel, searched out by Arioch, enters the picture.

You may wish to note that the first six chapters of Daniel contain exceptionally well-crafted stories and that their literary impact appears to be part of the author's intent. It may even be the case that details are added or omitted simply to increase the effectiveness of a particular story. Literary observations along these lines may help to answer a lot of questions, such as *Why didn't Daniel do this . . . ?* or *Why didn't the king do that . . . ?*

God's Help Is Easy to Find

Daniel had obviously formed a good relationship with the king's officials, and, as we also learn, with the king himself. Following the king's command, Arioch probably could have lopped off Daniel's head as soon as he found him, but instead he took the time to answer Daniel's question about why the king was so enraged.

Have the group take careful note of the steps Daniel takes as he faces this crisis. First, he dares to approach the king—the root of the problem—to ask for time. It must have taken phenomenal faith on Daniel's part to even suggest to the king that he, Daniel, would be able to interpret the dream when everyone else had failed. If the king had been enraged with his customary advisers, imagine how impatient he could be with this foreign-born wise-man-in-training!

Second, Daniel tells his three friends about the problem. We often fall into the habit of keeping our problems to ourselves, not wanting to burden anyone else with them, but this is not the example we see in Daniel. He explains everything to his close friends so that they can join him in the next step.

Third, Daniel urges his friends to "plead for mercy from the God of heaven" (2:18). Daniel and his friends take prayer seriously, knowing that it gives them direct access to the Lord God of heaven and earth, who listens (1 Kings 8:27-28). And during the night, after Daniel and his friends have prayed, God reveals to Daniel both the dream and its meaning.

Thus equipped, and before returning to the king, Daniel demonstrates an important fourth step in his approach to this crisis. He thanks God (Dan. 2:20-23). Daniel's words of praise and thanksgiving in this follow-up prayer make a beautiful model for anyone who has received an answer from God.

The Dream and Its Details

As you begin to talk about Nebuchadnezzar's dream, be aware that at least some group members may struggle with the somewhat complicated details and the historical events they appear to represent. No, we don't usually talk much about the history of the intertestamental period. But that's all the more reason to encourage people to gain at least a basic understanding of events that followed the Babylonian captivity and the eventual return to Jerusalem. Make sure the group understands that a basic knowledge of this period is critical to making sense of the second half of the book of Daniel as well as other books in the Bible.

With a few visual aids—especially if you can make use of them from session to session—this basic level of understanding shouldn't be hard to achieve. As the Additional Notes on Daniel 2:31-43 in the study guide point out, there are really only four kingdoms to keep in mind: Babylon, Medo-Persia, Greece (including divisions of the Greek Empire after Alexander's death), and Rome. Within each kingdom, there are only a few leaders who figure prominently: in Babylon, there's Nebuchadnezzar and his descendant Belshazzar; in the Medo-Persian Empire, there's Darius the Mede and Cyrus the Persian; in the Greek Empire, there's Alexander the Great and two of the generals who succeeded him: Ptolemy and Seleucus (and their descendants); and for Rome, no individual leaders are highlighted in Daniel's prophecies. A rudimentary understanding of these four kingdoms and their leaders will make all of Daniel—especially the second half—far more enjoyable.

The statue in Nebuchadnezzar's dream serves as a great visual aid for learning these kingdoms: the golden head represents Babylon; the silver chest and arms, Medo-Persia; the bronze belly and thighs, Greece; and the legs of iron and feet of iron and clay, Rome.

Of more interest to the group may be the rock that "was cut out, but not by human hands" (2:34). Appearing as it did during the reign of Rome, it seems almost certain that this is a reference to Jesus and the ultimate victory he would achieve over every other kingdom (2:44-45). Even if this is all that group members remember from Daniel's prophecy, at least they'll go away remembering the most important kingdom!

All's Well That Ends with a Promotion

The ever-surprising King Nebuchadnezzar responds to Daniel's interpretation of the dream in exactly the way the author wants us to respond: not with amazement for Daniel's abilities but with praise and honor for God. Just as the king acknowledges "the God of gods and the Lord of kings," so the writer wants us to know that God, not the prophet, is the one who has solved the mystery of the dream and its interpretation.

The end of the story also follows a pattern often found in dream stories: the hero receives a reward that somehow shows he is better off than at the beginning of the story. Like Daniel, if we have learned to turn to God when faced with a troubling situation, then we too have come to the end of this story better off than when we started!

GENERAL DISCUSSION

1. In the Scriptures, dreams often have significant meanings (consider the dreams of Jacob, Joseph, Solomon, and Joseph, the adoptive father of Jesus). Does God still speak through dreams today? Have we been neglecting an avenue of God's communication?

This question is probably more difficult than it seems at first. Some people may want to quickly say that God's visions were for biblical times and that it's nonsense to think God still speaks to people in dreams. But there's every possibility that someone in your study group will describe an incident in which they believe they were visited by God or an angel in a dream. (I myself had a visitation experience after witnessing the death of a seven-year-old girl in a car accident; I've also listened to dozens of dream stories during my ministry.)

Here's how I would approach this answer: First, take note of biblical examples. Jacob saw a ladder reaching to heaven (Gen. 28:12-15); Joseph dreamed about sheaves of wheat and stars in the sky (37:5-9); Solomon dreamed about asking for wisdom (1 Kings 3:5-15); Joseph was visited by an angel who told him to take Mary as his wife (Matt. 1:20-24).

In each case, consider the purpose of the dream (renewal of the covenant, a glimpse of the future, granting a special gift, giving direction), and reflect on whether God can accomplish these same purposes today using other means. After a bit of discussion, the answer you want to come to is that God can accomplish many of these same purposes through God's Word, the Bible.

We have an extraordinary gift in the Bible, and through it God is able to communicate with us in every situation. If we're waiting for God to come to us in the night, we might do well to pick up God's Word while we're still awake. The answers we seek are probably there.

This does not rule out the possibility of God's sending dreams and visions for unique circumstances, as the Lord did for Nebuchadnezzar. It may be that we quickly discount the dreams we experience. But in cases of dreams we remember well, we may want to test them against God's Word. Is the message consistent with the Bible? Does the dream honor God? Does the dream serve a biblical purpose? If the answer to any of these questions is no, I'd suggest that the dream was not so much a message from God as a reminder to seek clear communication from God's Word.

2. *Nebuchadnezzar's wise men could not give him the answers he wanted. In what kinds of contemporary situations do people turn to "wise ones" or "experts" for answers when they should be turning to God and God's servants instead?*

After group members have reflected for a few moments, they will probably fire off a fusillade of answers. Here are just a few examples they might mention:

- politicians taking advice from lobbyists
- people with assorted problems (health, finances, relationships) calling in to radio or TV programs, writing to advice columnists, or consulting psychics
- teenagers soliciting advice from their peers
- ministers who preach the latest wisdom of popular writers rather than beginning with God's Word

Our society these days has a tremendous number of "helping" professionals, not many of whom are trained in God's wisdom. These professionals have their place, and God can use them to accomplish good things, but we should remember to begin our search for answers by seeking out God and God's servants.

In your discussion you may also want to bring up the issue of trusting in God *versus* seeking professional help. Many well-intentioned people, after petitioning God in prayer, refuse to consider the possibility that God is answering their prayers by sending help through professional counselors or consultants.

You may want to remind the group of the story about the man who asked God for help when he was caught on his roof during a flood. When a neighbor in a rowboat came by, asking if he needed assistance, the stranded man said, "No, my God is going to help me." When a canoe came by, the man on the roof said the same thing. When a helicopter offered to pluck him out of the water, he again said God was going to rescue him. After the man died in the flood and went to heaven, he asked God why he didn't come to save him—to which God answered, "What do you mean? I sent you a rowboat, a canoe, and a helicopter!" We too need to be ready to take advantage of the help God offers after we have gone to the Lord in prayer.

3. *How important was prayer as Daniel sought an answer for the king?*

A careful reading of Daniel 2:17-18 reveals Daniel's thoughts about prayer in dealing with this crisis. (See the section "God's Help Is Easy to Find" in the preceding leader's notes.) Can you imagine Daniel's friends' reaction when they hear they need to ask God not only for the meaning of the king's dream but also for the dream itself? It doesn't seem to matter to Daniel that what he's asking for is unprecedented, but he knows he wants his friends to help him in bringing this unusual request before God.

Notice also the use of strong words in the description of Daniel's actions. *Urging* conveys more of a sense of importance than merely *asking* or *inviting* his friends to pray along. *Pleading* is another strong word. It conveys a sense of one's helplessness before God. Daniel wasn't simply asking or requesting an answer from God; he was pleading for his and others' lives. It seems pretty obvious that Daniel knew this dream challenge was something he could not accomplish on his own. God alone had the answer Daniel needed, and Daniel was willing to plead for it.

Daniel and his friends plead for *mercy*. They know God can grant them their petition, and yet they know God doesn't owe them any favors. It is God's prerogative to give mercy; Daniel and his friends know they cannot lay claim to it. But they also know that they can ask—and that God hears.

Clearly prayer is of life-and-death importance to Daniel and his friends.

4. *Daniel told the king that the statue in his dream represented a succession of kingdoms. Wouldn't most despots be enraged to*

hear that their kingdoms would be superseded? What does it say about Nebuchadnezzar that he took this news so calmly?

As we will see in the next few lessons of this study, it's hard to know just what Nebuchadnezzar will do next. One day he's destroying Jerusalem; the next day he's praising the God of Israel. Nebuchadnezzar is certainly one of the more complex individuals we meet in God's Word.

In Daniel 1 we read that the king calmly orders his new captives—from the Jewish nobility—to be trained in the language and literature of Babylon. Most despots would have ordered that anyone associated with the royalty of a conquered nation be immediately put to death. In Daniel 2, Nebuchadnezzar becomes enraged by his hapless advisers, ordering their death. This volatile side of his personality appears again in the account of the fiery furnace (Dan. 3:13, 19). Then again, as we learn in Daniel 4, Nebuchadnezzar relates calmly and rationally his story of another dream that points to his going insane for a while and describes how his sanity and kingly power are eventually restored.

The most valuable insight from discussing this question may be the realization that people can and do change—not all at once, and not often without some backsliding, but nonetheless with noticeable improvements. God had a plan, even for a volatile despot like Nebuchadnezzar, and we can see the working out of that plan as these stories progress. By the end of Daniel 4, when Nebuchadnezzar describes his becoming restored after his humiliation, his words of praise are as profound and sincere as those of any psalmist!

5. *Does it seem clear to you that the rock that was "cut out, but not by human hands" (Dan. 2:34), pointed to Jesus? Is the mountain that grew from this rock still growing in the world? Explain.*

It would be good to begin discussing this question by observing that we must always be on guard against reading too much into God's Word, especially if by our own cleverness we claim to "discover" prophecies or truths that God may not have intended to teach.

In this case, however, it seems pretty clear that the rock in Nebuchadnezzar's dream is a reference to the establishment of God's eternal kingdom through Jesus. We can be assured of this interpretation for several reasons.

First, it's consistent with the message of other parts of the Bible. We should see a red flag anytime we encounter an interpretation of one passage that is inconsistent with that of other, similar passages. In this case, the reference to the rock is consistent with the message of the kingdom of God throughout the New Testament.

Second, the interpretation has been borne out in history. The very existence of the Christian church today is evidence of the continuing growth of God's kingdom throughout this world. We can also note that the test of a true prophet is whether one's prophecy comes to pass (Deut. 18:21-22).

Finally, unlike some passages in which several plausible interpretations are possible, there is no alternate interpretation that might cause us to question whether the rock in this passage points to the coming of God's kingdom through Jesus.

As far as the growth of the mountain today is concerned, yes, the kingdom of God continues to increase in influence around the world. A quick review of Internet statistics regarding the Christian faith (taking into account that some sites are more trustworthy than others) reveals a consistent and remarkable growth trend in Christianity worldwide. If time allows, you might want to discuss why this growth trend appears to have stalled and may even be reversing in North America.

SMALL GROUP SESSION IDEAS

Opening (10 minutes)

Take time to welcome anyone who may be new to your group or to this study. Ask if any questions have come up since the previous lesson. Also, if anyone has been working on a special project related to this study—such as researching a character from Daniel, or preparing a time line—take some time to share the results now or perhaps at another time during this session.

Prayer—Consider together how Daniel and his companions must have felt as they spent the night in prayer, asking for God's mercy so that their lives would be spared. Then read Psalm 130 before spending a few moments in prayer, asking for God's wisdom and understanding in your study of this lesson.

Share—Mostly for fun, but possibly for insight as well, ask if anyone in the group has had a dream he or she clearly remembers. If no one remembers a specific dream, ask about the kinds of dreams people in the group may have experienced (some common themes include flying, falling, or being unprepared for an important event). Take care to be sensitive in commenting on what people share.

Focus—This lesson examines the mystery of Nebuchadnezzar's dream, Daniel's faithfulness in believing that God would reveal both the dream and its meaning, and an important prophecy about God's eternal kingdom. Keep this question in mind as you work through this lesson: *How can faith in God make me better able to help others learn about the one true God?*

Growing (35-40 minutes)
Read—It could take several minutes to read Daniel 2 out loud, so you may wish to ask group members to summarize the story in sequence (*What happened first? Okay, what happened after that?* and so on.) Just make sure to cover all the important parts!

Discuss—Use the following questions to go deeper on various topics while working through the General Discussion questions.

- Who are today's volatile tyrants? Should we limit our thinking to the leaders of nations, or are there other tyrants who also control the course of people's lives? Explain.

- How do today's religious and spiritual leaders rank in the world's view regarding people who have the gift of wisdom? In your view?

- Nebuchadnezzar was told that his kingdom would be followed by several others. Will the "kingdoms" of the United States, Canada, and other democratic nations last forever? What role will spiritual wisdom play in their continued existence?

- The rock in Nebuchadnezzar's dream proved to be more powerful than any empire represented in the great statue. What are some of the little ways in which faith proves to be stronger than the world's greatest powers?

Goalsetting (5 minutes)
Invite group members to pray daily for themselves and for each other, specifically asking God to give them wisdom in their daily living. Then begin your next session by asking group members to tell about ways in which they've experienced God's answers to those prayers. (It may be helpful to hand out a small prayer reminder such as Daniel 2:20-23 printed on a small card.)

Closing (10 minutes)
Preparing for Prayer—If group members are willing, invite them to share their thoughts on specific areas in their lives in which

they are seeking wisdom and discernment (see Goalsetting above). What "mysteries" would they like to see answered? Also ask if people have particular praises or concerns they'd like others to pray about.

Prayer—Remembering Nebuchadnezzar's threats and Daniel's faithfulness, begin your closing prayer with a reading of Psalm 141. Then continue in prayer by asking people to join in with specific requests that have been mentioned. Ask also that God's blessings of wisdom and faithfulness may become more and more a part of everyone's daily living.

Group Study Project (Optional)
The Bible contains many stories about dreams and dreamers. Any group members who want to dig deeper into this subject may wish to compare one or two other dream stories with the one they've looked at in this lesson. Then perhaps they could report on their findings during another lesson that deals with a dream, such as lesson 4.

3

DANIEL 3

A Blaze of Glory

In a Nutshell

Daniel disappears from center stage briefly while his three friends show their faith by refusing to worship an image of gold. Their confidence and God's protection of them result in another confession of God's greatness by the king of Babylon. The friends also demonstrate the importance of not compromising on matters of faith.

Appearances Are Deceiving

It may seem at first that this lesson on the story of the fiery furnace should be easy to lead. As with the story about the lions' den (Dan. 6), there's hardly a need to deal with Babylonian history or mysterious dreams and visions, and the narrative moves forward as crisply as any movie plot. But when it comes to applying the story's teachings to our own lives, we may find this one of the more challenging lessons in the book of Daniel.

Consider rising to the challenge by asking some questions like these: *Of the problems we've encountered so far in Daniel, which are we most likely to confront today? Adhering to dietary laws while exiled in a foreign land? Interpreting dreams for a violent tyrant? Or being tempted to compromise our faith by bowing down to a false god, which* everyone *else is doing?* It may take a few moments for group members to come to this realization, but this story in Daniel strikes at the heart of our everyday living.

It's no accident that Nebuchadnezzar's statue on the plain of Dura was huge and easily seen; many of the greatest challenges to our faith today—casual immorality, self-serving greed, corrupted values—are equally at the center of our culture's attention. Neither is it a coincidence that Nebuchadnezzar's statue was made of gold. Money and wealth may be the most aggressive false gods of all! If you and your group are able to connect with Daniel's friends in the challenge they faced on the plain of Dura, this may be one of the most eye-opening lessons in your study of Daniel.

One aspect of this story that may help bring it closer to home is that it involves ordinary heroes. As the study guide points out, Daniel is absent, and we aren't told why. But that presents a wonderful teaching opportunity. The heroes of this story are relatively unknown—and thus more like everyday, ordinary people with whom most of us can identify.

You may want to ask your group how their reaction to the story might have been if Daniel, rather than his lesser-known friends, had remained standing while everyone else bowed down. This story goes a long way in helping us see that ordinary people can do extraordinary things when they place their trust in God.

Setting the Stage for Conflict

Nebuchadnezzar inadvertently set the stage for conflict when he set up his enormous statue. For political reasons he was probably trying to unify the worship of his far-flung empire around a common deity. It may also be that this statue was intended as a pilgrimage destination. Encouraging everyone to visit a particular place is an effective way to create a sense of unity. In light of these thoughts, you might ask group members, *How do people feel about their country after they've visited the capitol and all its monuments? Why are there often so many monuments there? Similarly, why are all Muslims required to visit Mecca once in their lives? Or Mormons to visit Palmyra, New York?*

Once the statue was set up and the people had gathered, the herald announced the day's program: There would be some music, followed by much falling down and worshiping of the golden image. And for any people who didn't participate, a living cremation awaited them in the king's furnace.

Again, the parallels to today's faith challenges are fairly clear. The key word is *everyone*. Just as *everyone* was expected to bow down to the king's statue, so *everyone* today is called to participate in immoral behavior, *everyone* is urged to go after wealth and money, and *everyone* is told to indulge in self-centered attitudes and behaviors.

No, Not Everyone

Well, as we learn, not *everyone* does these things. When we look out across the plain of Dura, we can see three people still standing: Shadrach, Meshach, and Abednego. In some ways, this is the most powerful part of the lesson, even greater than the miraculous protection from the flames. We already know that God can work miracles, but how confident are we that three ordinary people can make a stand against an entire empire of people bowing to a false god?

If we had any doubts, the example of these three believers shows us that we too can stand. We do not have to compromise our faith simply because so many other people are willing to bow down. We can stand firm for what we believe.

The Heat Is On

Evil does not take kindly to being defied. Like Shadrach, Meshach, and Abednego, we too can expect to take heat for daring to stand up in obedience to our God.

The march to the furnace marks the peak of the conflict in this story. After the three friends are given a second chance to bow down (building the suspense, and thus giving the three a chance to add some foreshadowing), the narrator tells us that the king wants his furnace heated "seven times hotter than usual" (Dan. 3:19). Be sure not to miss the theological significance of that number *seven*—often used in the Bible to mean completeness or perfection. In other words, God can protect us even from something that is completely evil. Even the most perfect power of destruction cannot harm those who have faith in God.

As the suspense builds, more fascinating things happen, and if we haven't heard the story before, we can't help being amazed at what happens in the furnace. Though three men have gone in, suddenly there are four—and not one of them is being burned alive!

So Nebuchadnezzar calls the men out, and soon they are surrounded by the crowd of idol worshipers, who can see that not so much as a "hair of their heads" has been singed (3:27). Not even the smell of the fire clings to them. This is another key point. Not even the aroma of evil can linger on those who place their faith in God. The Lord will keep them perfectly safe, pure, and unharmed—if not here and now, then surely in eternity (note 3:17-18 again, and look ahead to 12:1-2).

GENERAL DISCUSSION

1. *Nebuchadnezzar was apparently trying to unify a diverse kingdom around the worship of a new common god. Is religion an effective way to bring diverse groups of people together? What difference does it make if this happens by coercion or by choice?*

Some group members may be quick to point out that the United States, Canada, and many other countries have been founded on principles that allow religious freedom rather than forcing citizens to follow one religion or to worship one deity. But there are still many nations in the world where citizens are expected to adhere to a common faith. Many predominantly Muslim countries, for example, are already governed as theocracies; others are moving in that direction.

If you have a knack for playing devil's advocate, you may wish to pose this question: *If we are convinced that our faith is the one true way to salvation, why* not *make it the law of the land?* After all, wouldn't our nation be a better place to live if everyone grew up with a common belief in a loving, faithful God?

The point, of course, is that you cannot coerce true faith. You can force people into performing rituals; you can get them to conform to customs; you may even be able to get them to say all the right words or entice them to make pilgrimages to seek out special blessings. But you cannot mandate what someone believes in his or her heart. Faith confessed at the tip of a sword (or at the door of a fiery furnace) is not likely to be true faith.

Look again at the first part of this discussion question: *Is religion an effective way to bring diverse groups of people together?* Apart from coercion, the Christian religion and worldview, based on God's covenantal, kingdom vision for us to live in unity with each other and the Lord, is the best way to bridge gaps between culture, ethnicity, nationality, and even language. Many of the common beliefs and practices of the Christian faith can unite people who otherwise have little in common.

In some parts of the world where there is constant conflict—such as the Middle East—faith in the one true God (not Allah) may be the only hope of ever bringing together warring factions. When we accept the Prince of Peace as our common Savior, we begin to realize that all other differences that divide us are of little consequence.

2. *Based on what we know from just the first three chapters of Daniel, why do you think Shadrach, Meshach, and Abednego refused to bow down?*

This is what we might call an opinion question, one that's intended to help people identify personally with the faith motivation behind the actions chosen by Daniel's three friends. You may want to begin by asking the group whether it's easy or hard to be the only person in a group who thinks or acts in a particular way. Think of popular fashions, fads, music, slang, and ideals you've encountered at various times in your life. What is it about human nature that makes us want to go along with the group, even if it makes us uncomfortable?

As noted earlier in the section "Appearances Are Deceiving," we have very little information in Daniel about Shadrach, Meshach, and Abednego. They are named and renamed in Daniel 1; they joined with Daniel in refusing the king's rich food while they were being trained in Babylon; together with Daniel they received "knowledge and understanding of all kinds of literature and learning" from God (Dan. 1:17); they also prayed with Daniel when he asked God to reveal and help him understand the king's dream (2:17-19). Beyond that, all we know is that the friends had become "administrators over the province of Babylon" (2:49; 3:12) and that they refused to bow down to the king's statue.

A few clues about their decision-making process become apparent when the king gave them a second chance to worship his idol (3:16-18). The first thing the three of them said was that they did not need to defend their decision before Nebuchadnezzar. In other words, their first allegiance was to God. This is a significant point. If we always put God in first place, faith decisions are much easier to make. It won't be as hard to think or act differently on account of our faith if we always make trusting in God our first priority.

Shadrach, Meshach, and Abednego next told the king that even if he threw them into the furnace, their God could rescue them. This is an acknowledgment of God's power to save, almost certainly based on their experience with God since arriving in Babylon. They had survived the food test and were healthier than any of the other young men; they had seen Daniel receive the interpretation of the king's dream; and they now believed that God could save them from the furnace.

This might be a good time to introduce the question of why God sometimes saves his servants from execution and other times allows them to die for their faith. Consider Stephen in Acts 7; why didn't God rescue him from being stoned? Did God rescue Daniel's friends for their own sakes, or was it perhaps for Nebuchadnezzar's benefit, or some other reason? (Your discussion of question 3 can pick up on this matter also).

Further, Daniel's friends told Nebuchadnezzar that even though God might not rescue them from the fire, they still wouldn't worship the king's image of gold. Some scholars comment that this quote may have been included as an encouragement and a comfort to people of later years who found themselves living under severe persecution, challenged to bow down to every kind of abomination in defiance of God (see 9:27 and 11:31, most likely references to Antiochus IV Epiphanes, a cruel oppressor of the Jews in the second century B.C.).

Ultimately the best answer to why Shadrach, Meshach, and Abednego refused to bow down is the simplest: *They had faith in God.* Whether they lived or died, they believed their faith would not be disappointed.

3. *Would this story's lesson about uncompromising faith have been any different if the three friends had died in the fire? Why or why not?*

History is filled with examples of people who were not miraculously rescued from fires, stonings, drownings, or other executions for their faith in God. This doesn't mean God was absent or uncaring in any of those situations; it simply means God works in ways that are often beyond our ability to comprehend. It's often after the fact—sometimes many years later—that we begin to see how God has shown mercy even in the act of allowing faithful believers to suffer and die.

Directing your group's discussion of this question calls for some sensitivity. Someone who is still new to the Christian faith may want to see a direct connection between faith and deliverance, while someone who is more seasoned in faith will understand that God's will could be accomplished whether the three men survived or perished in the furnace.

Shadrach, Meshach, and Abednego themselves made clear that they knew they might not be rescued—and that whatever happened, they would stand up to Nebuchadnezzar's idol (3:16-18). Later generations of believers who have turned to the book of Daniel for wisdom and encouragement have certainly known that not everyone will be spared from execution (see Heb. 11:35-40).

Here's the difficult but important bottom line on this discussion: *If we choose to live by faith only as long as we see direct benefits from our choice (such as being rescued from the furnace after refusing to bow to an idol), then we won't live by faith for very long.* Often in our lives we will not see immediate answers to prayer, we will not receive angelic visitors in a time of trial, and we will not walk away from the fiery furnace unsinged. When we refuse to compromise our faith in such situations, we truly begin to show the world what faith is about. "Faith is being sure of what we hope for and certain of what we do not see" (Heb. 11:1). If Nebuchadnezzar's furnace had claimed three more victims, this story might not have had so exciting an ending, but its lesson about uncompromising faith would have been no different.

4. *God's angels are messengers (our word* angel *comes from the Greek word* angelos, *meaning "messenger"). What message might the angel in the furnace have been bringing?*

In this story it's actually quite surprising to see how little is made of the fact that a heavenly being appeared in the fire with Daniel's friends. Lesson 8 of this study deals with the subject of the heavenly beings who visited Daniel, so if you're pressed for time you may wish to defer this discussion until you study that lesson. Or perhaps you'd like to take just a few minutes here to introduce the subject and mention that lesson 8 will offer a more in-depth discussion on angels.

As the study guide points out, it has often been suggested that the fourth person who appeared in the fire was actually Jesus. But no clear reason is given to believe this is so—other than Nebuchadnezzar's observation that the fourth person in the fire looked "like a son of the gods" (3:25), a description that could also refer to an angel.

Neither do we have any evidence for what message, if any, an angel might have been delivering to Shadrach, Meshach, and Abednego. The fact that an angel was sent, though, conveys the message that God was watching over his servants, even in their exile far from home. This would have been an important message of encouragement to persecuted believers who read the book of Daniel in later years.

One message the angel may well have brought to the three men in the furnace isn't recorded in Daniel but is often the first thing an angel says in an encounter with a human being: "Do not be afraid!" (see 10:12, for example). But, then again, simply the presence of God's angel could have clearly conveyed that message to the three friends.

You may wish to close this discussion by identifying some of the things that cause us to be afraid today. How does God convey to us that we need not be afraid?

5. *Nebuchadnezzar praised God again at the end of this story. He also threatened to kill anyone who said anything against the God*

of the Jews. Do you think the king believed his own words of praise? What might have been a better response than the threat he delivered?

The point of this question is to convey that God didn't need Nebuchadnezzar's murderous help to protect the honor of the divine holy name. The fact that Nebuchadnezzar responded to God's deliverance of the three friends with a threat of more violence showed that he was still impressed with his own status and power—and not sufficiently impressed with God's power.

In the same way, we often respond to God's grace in our lives with a sense of self-importance rather than humility. Consider raising this point in your group discussion: Many believers in North America are among the world's most prosperous people. We know we have been delivered from our sins and spared from an eternal fiery furnace. Yet our response is often not one of humble submission before God but one of entitlement. We don't say as much in words—no, we praise God as Nebuchadnezzar did—but how often don't our actions say, "I'm really something; look at my important job, my big house, my designer clothes, my powerful, new car," and so on. Like Nebuchadnezzar, we often respond to God's grace in not-so-humble ways. God does not want or need us to demonstrate power (think *buying power,* for example) but humility and obedience.

"What does the LORD require of you? To act justly and to love mercy and to walk humbly with your God" (Mic. 6:8). This is the response God desires for showing us mercy. God doesn't need our boasting about how powerful or smart or capable we are. God's power is sufficient—and we wouldn't even have power or smarts or other abilities if God hadn't given them to us (John 19:11; James 1:17). Rather than issuing a threat to turn people's houses into piles of rubble, it would have been better if Nebuchadnezzar had allowed his own self-importance to be broken.

SMALL GROUP SESSION IDEAS

Opening (10 minutes)

Welcome anyone who may be new to the group. Repeating names or simple introductions can be helpful.

As a follow-up to the goalsetting exercise from session 2, ask group members about the "prayer for wisdom" challenge. Did anyone experience a gift of wisdom or insight since the group met for that session? Some members may have some interesting and surprising responses. If not, though, encourage everyone to keep praying for each other. God's timing is not always what we want or expect it to be.

Prayer—Read Habakkuk 3:17-18, noting that Habakkuk was a prophet who served God in the days when Daniel and his friends were growing up in Jerusalem (around 600 B.C.). Note also the willingness of Habakkuk to place his unwavering trust in God, even if all the signs he hoped for did not come to pass. Pray together that this time of study will help everyone develop a faith that's strong enough to praise God even when things don't go the way we might want them to.

Share—Ask if anyone studied dreams and dreamers as suggested in the study project at the end of session 2. If so, allow time for people to share what they've learned. If no one did the optional study, move into a general, but brief, discussion about compromise: *When is compromise a good thing? When is it wrong?*

Focus—Shadrach, Meshach, and Abednego were not willing to bow down to a false god—not even when their lives were on the line. Keep this question in mind as you discuss this lesson: *What are some ways in which I have compromised instead of standing up for my faith?*

Growing (35-40 minutes)
Read—Of all the stories in Daniel, this one has the clearest ties to oral tradition. Suggest that someone read the chapter expressively—with plenty of emphasis on the numerous lists and repetitions—while the rest of the group listens (rather than reading along). After the reading, you might ask if people heard anything in the telling of the story that they hadn't noticed while reading it before.

Discuss—Use the following questions along with the General Discussion questions to help you think about uncompromising faith.

• Rather than giant statues, today's idols can be ideas, trends, personalities, lifestyles, material goods, addictions, and more. What are some of the specific idols that people are urged or maybe even forced to bow down to today? What is society's attitude toward people who refuse to bow down?

• Name a time when someone you know (or know of) stood up for his or her faith. What impression did it leave on you?

- The astrologers in the story were quick to point out that Shadrach, Meshach, and Abednego refused to bow down. Why do many people see strong faith as a threat? Is it easier to get along with people if we compromise instead of standing firm? Explain.

- Throughout history, people of faith have faced many kinds of persecution. Do we still face "fiery furnaces" today? If so, what are they? If not, what does that say about our faith?

Goalsetting (5 minutes)
Changing from compromise to unyielding commitment is not easy! Encourage group members to be watchful of times in the coming week when they may be tempted to compromise their faith. Some may even want to jot down a few notes about incidents that occur. Ask everyone also to note examples of people who are standing firm in their faith.

Closing (10 minutes)
Preparing for Prayer—Not everyone gets an angelic visitor when tempted to bow down to a false god—but God does send other messengers to give us strength. Take a few moments to reflect together on some of the ways God may send us strength and encouragement to stand up for our faith in our day-to-day living. Also invite people to mention praises and concerns they'd like the group to pray about.

Prayer—Encourage group members to pray for themselves and others, asking specifically for the courage to stand up when everyone else is bowing down. Remember also to pray for specific concerns that have been raised during this study session. Close, if you like, by reading a praise passage about God's protection, such as Psalm 121 or 124, or by singing a doxology such as "Now Blessed Be the Lord Our God."

Group Study Project (Optional)
The persecution of believers in God is not merely a historical subject; it continues today. Some of your group members may be interested in gathering information about persecuted believers. It may be a real eye-opener to learn about the number of people who face "fiery furnaces" today.

4

DANIEL 4

Pride and Punishment

In a Nutshell

Madness descends on prideful King Nebuchadnezzar as his education about the God of Israel continues (a prominent theme in the first few chapters of Daniel). As we observe the king in his humiliation and restoration, we are reminded that arrogant pride has no place in the life of anyone called to worship and serve God. We also learn that even the bitterest enemy of God's people can learn to sing God's praises.

A Change of Perspective

Having used several different literary devices in the first three chapters, the writer of Daniel now uses a flashback to illustrate a lesson about pride. The author also brings in Nebuchadnezzar to tell the story in his own words, creating the strong impact of a first-person narrative that includes a personal testimony of belief in God.

We notice immediately that there seems to be something different about the king. All the venom seems to have been drained out of his system as he begins: "It is my pleasure to tell you about the miraculous signs and wonders that the Most High God has performed for me" (Dan. 4:2). Is this really Nebuchadnezzar, the tyrant who destroyed Jerusalem, who ordered all his own wise men killed, and who tried to incinerate Shadrach, Meshach, and Abednego? What happened to that tyrant?

That's what the story in Daniel 4 is all about. Nebuchadnezzar wants to tell us, in his own words, how the God of Israel finally got through to him. You may find that in some ways this lesson is not an easy one to lead, because few, if any, of us like being reminded that we may need to be humbled.

1) Welcome

Leopards No, People Yes

It may be helpful to begin your group study of this lesson with a general discussion of how people can change—or even *if* people can change. For example, you could toss out a saying like "A leopard can't change its spots" or "You can't teach an old dog new tricks" and see how people react. Should Christians believe such statements are true? If the answer is no, what does it take for people to change, especially people who are locked into patterns of negative behavior?

Often it takes a particularly humbling experience, some kind of journey to rock-bottom in which a person is finally forced to admit that he or she is unable to change without the help of God. Maybe some in your group have experienced that kind of humbling journey. If they're willing to share their stories, give them as much time as they need. As we learn from Nebuchadnezzar's story, there's nothing like a first-person account to teach us valuable lessons.

Anyone ?

3) Read Psa 145:1-13a Prayer

King Insomnia

This episode includes no time marker (compare, for example, the opening verses of Dan. 1-2, 7-10), so we can't say exactly when this story takes place during the reign of Nebuchadnezzar. All we know is that it's sometime after the stories recounted in Daniel 1-3 and sometime before a period of restoration and blessing in Nebuchadnezzar's reign (4:36), which ended in 562 B.C.. The archaeological record offers no clue as to when the king may have been absent from his throne for a time, which may have been as long as seven years ("seven times"—4:23). But that silence shouldn't cause us to question the truth of the story in Daniel. After all, a period of insanity is hardly the kind of thing a king would want in the public record of his reign!

At the opening of Nebuchadnezzar's story, all was well. He was at home in his palace, "contented and prosperous" (4:4). But then in the midst of this serenity the king experienced a dream that "made [him] afraid" (4:5). You might want to ask group members if they've had a similar experience. Can we usually see difficult situations coming, like a train bearing down on us from a distance? Or do crises take us by surprise when we think all is peaceful? What can such experiences teach us about the need to be watchful and prepared in our lives?

(4) ?

When Daniel was eventually summoned to interpret the dream, he was perplexed by it "for a time, and his thoughts terrified him" (4:19). We don't know how long Daniel reflected on the dream before telling Nebuchadnezzar its meaning, but WHY? the fact that it terrified him probably showed on his face, for the king said, "Belteshazzar, do not let the dream or its meaning alarm you" (4:19). Perhaps what terrified Daniel was that he knew he was being called to bear bad news to the king—and we know that sometimes kings don't take kindly to bad news. Or maybe Daniel's terror sprang from wondering what would happen to both the king and the kingdom while Nebuchadnezzar was away from his throne. The picture of a huge tree being toppled surely meant devastating effects throughout the kingdom (4:14)—and perhaps Daniel, as chief of the king's advisers (2:48), would have an even greater burden of leadership than he already had.

Whatever Daniel's thoughts were, the king apparently was not surprised that the dream troubled Daniel. By now the king probably suspected that the dream spelled trouble. Eager to know the truth, however devastating it might be, the king pressed Daniel for the interpretation, even gently encouraging him.

A World-Spanning Tree

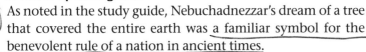

As noted in the study guide, Nebuchadnezzar's dream of a tree that covered the entire earth was a familiar symbol for the benevolent rule of a nation in ancient times.

You may wish to have a copy of Shel Silverstein's *The Giving Tree* handy for this part of the lesson. This children's book briefly and effectively illustrates why a tree is such a fitting symbol for the shelter and protection provided by a strong kingdom. On the basis of that symbol, consider taking a few minutes to ask some questions about the generous nature of God's kingdom.

Daniel confirmed what Nebuchadnezzar may have suspected, that his kingdom was somehow represented by the world-spanning tree. It was strong, had grown quickly, and had spread its branches to the ends of the earth. But all was not well with this kingdom. The messengers Nebuchadnezzar had seen "coming down from heaven" were saying, "Cut down the tree and trim off its branches; strip off its leaves and scatter its fruit. Let the animals flee from under it and the birds from its branches" (Dan. 4:13-14).

Deal or Warning?

After telling the king the interpretation of the dream, Daniel also dispensed some excellent advice, as noted in the study guide. Nebuchadnezzar faced a simple choice: *Continue to be wicked and suffer the consequences, or obey God and be spared.*

Someone in the group may observe that this offer sounds a lot like works-righteousness and that it appears Nebuchadnezzar is being offered a deal. We already know from the psalmist that God does not "repay us according to our iniquities" (Ps. 103:10), so why was Nebuchadnezzar offered this advice concerning his behavior? Does our prosperity also depend on our right behavior? If that's the case, why do we so often see the wicked prosper?

These are not easy questions. Note that in John 8:11 Jesus spares the woman caught in adultery but still tells her, "Go now and leave your life of sin" (John 8:11). The truth is that our behavior does matter to God, and sometimes we do suffer direct consequences as a result our actions—which is what Nebuchadnezzar was being told. Jeremiah and other prophets had delivered similar messages to God's people before they, in fact, were routed by Nebuchadnezzar. For example, when Jeremiah preached in the courtyard of the temple before the fall of Jerusalem, he declared, "The LORD sent me to prophesy against this house and this city all the things you have heard. Now reform your ways and your actions and obey the LORD your God. Then the LORD will relent and not bring the disaster he has pronounced against you" (Jer. 26:12-13).

Daniel was warning Nebuchadnezzar that he was nearing the end of his rope. Like a tipsy driver reaching for car keys, Nebuchadnezzar was drunk on his power, and Daniel was warning him not to take his fate into his own foolish hands.

Descent into Madness

When Nebuchadnezzar is sent out to live with animals, having lost his mind for speaking pridefully, we might wonder, *Of all the crimes for which Nebuchadnezzar could have been punished, was this truly the worst one?* Think about this question with your group, and consider how many other sins begin with some sort of pride—not to mention that pride is at the root of our breaking the greatest commandment—that we love the Lord" with all our heart, soul, mind, and strength (Mark12:29-30), placing God first in our lives (Ex. 20:1-8). Perhaps it's just when we think we're really something that we most need to be reminded how insignificant our power is compared to God's—and that it comes from God in the first place (John 19:11).

Restoration to Sanity

When God restored Nebuchadnezzar's sanity, the man glorified "the Most High" with eloquent words of praise (4:34). Notice the difference between these words of praise (4:34-35) and some others that we saw earlier (2:47; 3:28). How are they different? Would it be fair to say that Nebuchadnezzar now really meant what he was saying? Or perhaps that he now really knew what he was talking about? How can we tell?

In a brief epilogue (4:36-37) this story reports Nebuchadnezzar's return to his throne, but this does not mean, as in previous chapters of his life, a return to his old ways. Nebuchadnezzar himself declares, "Now I . . . praise and exalt and glorify the King of heaven, because everything he does is right and all his ways are just." Most important, the restored king accurately summarizes the entire story with a simple statement of why all this happened to him: "Those who walk in pride [the Lord] is able to humble" (4:37).

GENERAL DISCUSSION

1. *Why do you think the writer of Daniel casts Nebuchadnezzar as the first-person narrator of most of this story? What impact does that have on the reader?*

As we've already noticed in this study, the writer of Daniel is a master storyteller who uses a variety of literary devices and styles to convey important messages about faith in God. The shift from third-person narration to a first-person account catches our ears and perks up our interest just when our attention might be starting to fade.

Having Nebuchadnezzar speak is more than just a literary gimmick, however. Hearing the king tell this story in his own words gives us the sense that he truly "owns" it. This is no longer simply a story *about* Nebuchadnezzar; it's Nebuchadnezzar's story.

It's also worth noting that the king addresses his remarks to the entire world: "To the peoples, nations and men of every language, who live in all the world" (4:1). Nebuchadnezzar wants everyone to know his story and what God has done for him, and no matter where he goes, he can expect that people will hold him to his word.

The impact of this first-person narration can be compelling. For me, it lends an air of authenticity. For a few moments I forget that I am reading a 2,500-year-old document, and as the ancient king of Babylon uses the word "I,"

60 minutes

it seems as if he is speaking directly to me. His words become part of God's living Word.

While some excellent storytellers are truly gifted in telling someone else's story, the power of a first-person narrative can be striking—perhaps especially in live performance or on video. Television programs such as *60 Minutes* regularly allow people who are neither eloquent nor trained in public speaking to tell their own stories. Though they may stumble over their words and make grammatical errors, the fact that they are telling their own stories often makes their words riveting.

This is true for us too. Telling our own stories to others firsthand may be the best possible way to share our faith.

2. *How many significant trees can you think of that are mentioned in the Bible? Try to come up with five or more examples. What are some of the ways in which the kingdom of God is like a world-spanning tree?*

This exercise can add some fun as well as some insight into the story we're focusing on in this lesson. A concordance and a Bible dictionary will come in handy for an activity like this, so you might want to have these resources available. Here's a short list of some of the many biblical examples of trees people might mention:

- the tree of the knowledge of good and evil (Gen. 2:9)
- the tree of life (Gen. 2:9; Rev. 22:2)
- the great trees of Mamre (Gen. 13:18)
- the cedars of Lebanon (Judg. 9:15 and many other references)
- a tree planted by streams of water (Ps. 1:3)
- good trees bearing good fruit, bad trees bearing bad fruit (Matt. 7:17-20)
- a mustard tree (Matt. 13:31-32)
- a barren fig tree (Matt. 21:19)
- a sycamore tree (Luke 19:4)

In many of the numerous instances mentioned in Scripture, we find that if trees are flourishing, they give fruit, shelter, shade, oil, lumber, or some other benefit. These same qualities illustrate why the metaphor of a world-spanning tree is a fitting illustration for the kingdom of God. It stretches out over the entire earth, provides shelter for every kind of bird and animal, supplies food for all creatures, and protects them in many practical ways, bringing them together under the common care and good benefit of

God. In short, the tree is a fitting symbol of God's blessing and providence, resulting in the *shalom* intended for all things in God's kingdom.

Be aware that the image of a tree for a kingdom may be a new idea to some participants in your group. When you make the connection to the kingdom of God in Jesus' parable of the mustard seed, you may also want to refer back to Daniel 2, in which the kingdom of God is compared to a mountain that fills the entire earth. Which metaphor do you prefer? How does each picture teach different lessons about the kingdom of God?

3. *While walking on his palace roof, Nebuchadnezzar boasted about building the great city of Babylon. Do you think the king's boastful pride was enough of a reason for the punishment he received? Why or why not?*

When we think about the sin of pride, we can find ourselves wondering, *Which came first, the chicken or the egg? Does the sin of pride cause us to commit other sins, or do we commit other sins that lead us to prideful attitudes?* After a brief time of reflection, most people will see that the answer is *both*.

Nebuchadnezzar had lived a life characterized by all kinds of sin, so his prideful boasting was in some ways just another sin we could expect of someone who lived a godless life. But when we think about what being godless means— that is, placing something other than the one true God first in one's life, we can begin to see how pride runs deep at the root of human sin. Pride says, "No, I don't need God first in my life. I don't need to listen to God. I'm a lot more interested in doing what I want and putting what I like first in my life. After all, it's my life, and I'm going to live it the way I want to!" In other words, pride places the self and its desires ahead of God—and thus in the place of God—violating one's relationship with God and therefore all other relationships (with self, others, and creation) as well. (See Gen. 3:1-19; Ex. 20:3; Matt. 22:37-40). So even if Nebuchadnezzar had committed no other sin besides his prideful boast, it would have been enough to warrant the punishment he received—or far worse: total separation from God forever. One sin, actually, is enough to make us guilty of breaking all of God's law (James 2:10).

The Bible's teaching about sin and its devastating effects is hard, and sometimes we don't like to hear it. But thankfully the Bible also teaches about God's mercy and love,

49

especially in sending Jesus to deliver us from sin and give us new life empowered by the Spirit of God. Through this salvation we can live thankfully in right relationship with God, ourselves, others, and creation. Even before Jesus came, God offered mercy and forgiveness to people who repented and acknowledged the Lord (as Nebuchadnezzar did), and God credited it to them as righteousness (Rom. 4:1-11).

4. *Daniel advised Nebuchadnezzar to renounce his sins "by doing what is right" so that he might continue to prosper. Is this consistent with what we learn about faith, works, and blessings in the rest of the Bible? Do we win favor with God by doing what is right? Explain.*

It's safe to say that Nebuchadnezzar is probably not the best model for how Christians should live in relationship to God. Yes, Daniel told the king that he might forestall God's judgment by renouncing his sins and doing what is right, but Daniel never suggested that this could be a means to Nebuchadnezzar's salvation. In the same way, our faithful behavior today is pleasing to God, but it does not and cannot earn our salvation. Like Nebuchadnezzar, we too will slip; sin will take advantage of our slightest weakness.

What we see in Nebuchadnezzar is a good illustration of what the apostle Paul talks about in Romans 7. First, God's law teaches us to recognize our sin. Helping the king recognize the ways in which he was offending the one true God seems to have been part of Daniel's role in Babylon. Second, we realize we are unable to keep God's law perfectly, no matter how good our intentions. Finally, we recognize that we need to call on God for help.

Though we might try to win favor with God by living exceptionally good lives, the only way to receive salvation is through Jesus Christ, whose perfect life and sacrificial death for our sake earned salvation for us "once for all" (Heb. 10:10). Believing in God's power to save us through Jesus, rather than trying to save ourselves, is the only way. Because we're sinful, we'll never be good enough to live perfectly (Rom. 3:10, 23). We depend on the gift of God's grace for our salvation (3:21-30), and by the Spirit we live good lives in grateful response to God's mercy (2 Cor. 3:18; Eph. 2:8-10).

5. *What's significant about Nebuchadnezzar's becoming like a wild animal?*

The story of creation makes clear that only human beings are made in God's image. God told Adam and Eve, "Rule over the fish of the sea and the birds of the air and over every liv-ing creature that moves on the ground" (Gen. 1:28). King David recognized this same relationship between humanity and creation in Psalm 8:6-8: "You made him ruler over the works of your hands; you put everything under his feet: all flocks and herds, and the beasts of the field, the birds of the air, and the fish of the sea, all that swim the paths of the seas."

For Nebuchadnezzar to be reduced to the status of a wild animal was essentially a removal of his humanity. It's as if God were saying, "Since he lives like a beast, a beast he will become."

Animals, of course, cannot know their Creator in the same way God made possible for men and women. When we choose to live as if we are no wiser than animals, we deny our uniqueness in God's wonderful creation. We shouldn't deny the gifts God gave to animals (we can learn some wis-dom from them), but they are incapable of having a two-way, loving relationship with God. When, like Nebuchad-nezzar, we reduce our behavior to that of animals, we also make a mockery of our relationship with God.

6. *Do you think we will meet King Nebuchadnezzar in heaven?*

This question cannot be answered conclusively. It's included here only to stimulate some discussion about the transformation that took place in Nebuchadnezzar's life.

Consider that Nebuchadnezzar was God's instrument in carrying out judgment on the nation of Judah (Jer. 25:8-9; 27:6-7). When the devastation of Judah was complete, God could have simply abandoned the murderous tyrant who was concerned only about building his own kingdom. But God didn't abandon Nebuchadnezzar. God arranged for Daniel to be a servant in the king's palace; God troubled Nebuchadnezzar's sleep so that he learned to trust Daniel's wisdom; God showed Nebuchadnezzar his power in rescu-ing Daniel's friends from the fiery furnace; God also hum-bled Nebuchadnezzar by making him live like an animal for a time, when finally he acknowledged God as Most High.

Did God love Nebuchadnezzar? It certainly seems as if the answer is yes; God never let him go. The unanswered ques-tion is whether Nebuchadnezzar learned to truly love God. If we see him in heaven someday, we'll know the answer.

SMALL GROUP SESSION IDEAS

Opening (10 minutes)

Warmly welcome people who are new to the group. If you often have guests or newcomers, consider wearing nametags on a regular basis.

Discuss the goalsetting challenge from the previous session. Ask if group members were faced with the temptation to compromise their faith. If so, how did they meet that test?

At this point you may also want to ask people if they did the optional research project suggested at the end of session 3. If so, what did they learn about Christians facing persecution around the world?

Prayer—Begin your prayer time by reading together Psalm 145:1-13a. Then encourage group members to continue in silent prayer, asking God to use this lesson to help you identify areas in your lives that may be affected by sinful pride.

Share—To begin thinking about this lesson on Nebuchadnezzar's humiliation and restoration, ask if anyone is willing to share a humbling or embarrassing experience. What did he or she learn from it?

Focus—This lesson's main emphasis is about honoring God by giving up our pride, repenting of our sin, and living for the Lord who loves us and never lets us go. Keep the following question in mind as this lesson unfolds: *In what ways has my pride prevented me from praising and serving God?*

Growing (35-40 minutes)

Read—Once again, if you want to read the Scripture for this lesson during your session time, consider having the passage read aloud while others listen. Because Daniel 4 includes first-person narration (4:1-18, 34-37) and third-person narration (4:19-33), it could work well to have two people read the different parts.

Discuss—The following questions are intended to help us think personally about the dangerous reality of pride in our lives and how it affects the way we honor and serve God.

- What factors may have gone into making Nebuchadnezzar a prideful person? Which of these factors may be present in our own lives?

- Nebuchadnezzar called on Daniel to interpret God's messages for him. Does this still happen today? How can others help us discern what God is saying to us? Why is it that others can sometimes see God's messages more clearly than we can?

- How does God humble people today? Can you think of some widely known examples (consider people in government, business, religion, and so on). What effect do examples like these have on the general public?

- What do you think about the ending of Nebuchadnezzar's story, in which he receives greater power and prosperity than before? Can we expect that if we humble ourselves, God will give us greater blessings in our lives? Why or why not?

Goalsetting (5 minutes)

It's hard to recognize our own pride. Suggest setting a goal of looking in a mirror each day and asking God for the humility to see yourself as God sees you, as others see you, and as you should see yourself. Within the group, discuss other constructive ways in which we might identify pride in ourselves.

Closing (10 minutes)

Preparing for Prayer—No one wants to be humbled in the way Nebuchadnezzar was humbled. Invite the group to take a few moments to think silently about times when they deserved to be humbled but received mercy instead. If one or two people want to share their experience, invite them to do so. Group members should also feel free to mention other personal concerns and praises.

Prayer—Open your prayer time by reading Psalm 145:13b-21. Continue in prayer by thanking God for humbling experiences and for the mercy of forgiveness, salvation, and new life in Christ. Pray also for particular concerns and needs that have been mentioned.

Group Study Project (Optional)

Some or all of your group may be interested in writing a song in the style of Hannah's prayer (1 Sam. 2:1-10) or Mary's song (Luke 1:46-55), both of which convey a strong and moving message about pride and humility. Or perhaps they could try paraphrasing one of these songs by using contemporary words and images.

5

DANIEL 5

Heaven's Handwriting

In a Nutshell

When a disembodied hand appears and writes a cryptic message on the palace wall in Babylon, Daniel is again called in to solve a mystery. Though a different king is on the throne, the sin of pride remains the same, and God's message declares the end for Belshazzar and for the Babylonian Empire.

The meaning for us today? Those who are determined to defy God may also find their days numbered.

A Familiar Phrase

Nearly everyone knows what it means to "see the handwriting on the wall," though not as many know it comes from this story in Scripture. We still use this saying today to describe something that appears to be coming to an end, as in the case of a politician who is trailing far behind in the polls or a leading athlete whose career is beginning to fade.

As group leader, you can draw a connection between biblical history and life today by noting that just as we still use this familiar phrase based on an ancient Bible story, the lessons we find in that story, with its opening revelry, impetuous sacrilege, and incompetent spiritual advisers, still ring true today. People who play fast and loose and make a mockery of God, especially when they know better, will find their days numbered—often far sooner than they may think.

A Young King's Folly

There is excellent historical evidence indicating that King Belshazzar and his father, Nabonidus, were coregents in Babylon. Documents by the Babylonian historian Berossus (who wrote in Greek) as well as sources in cuneiform (a basalt pillar, a memorial inscription, and a stone tablet) tell us several key details about the life of Nabonidus, including the fact that he was known for his travels in Arabia. It may well have been during one of his absences that the story in Daniel 5 takes place.

The events of that fateful evening were set in motion when Belshazzar decided to host a banquet for a thousand of his nobles. The reason for this gathering is not specified, but we do know that Belshazzar and his guests were heavily drinking wine and that the king specifically ordered the gold and silver goblets from the temple in Jerusalem to be brought in so that everyone "might drink from them" (5:2). These were sacred objects intended for drink offerings that were part of the prescribed ritual in the Israelites' worship of God. The drink offerings are first mentioned in Exodus 29:38-40: "This is what you are to offer on the altar regularly each day: two lambs a year old. Offer one in the morning and the other at twilight. With the first lamb offer a tenth of an ephah of fine flour mixed with a quarter of a hin of oil from pressed olives, and a quarter of a hin of wine as a drink offering." Many other references to drink offerings are sprinkled throughout the Old Testament.

With your group you might consider what would happen in your local church if someone used the communion plate and cup in a way that mocked God. How would people react? What would be the consequences?

Even more important, you might ask why anyone would want to do such a thing. We find no reason given for Belshazzar's decision to profane the sacred vessels of the Jewish temple, but Daniel's comment in 5:23 makes clear that Belshazzar was committing a deliberate act of sacrilege.

We don't hear the word *sacrilege* used very often today. But perhaps you could consider together whether the following are examples of sacrilege:

- blatantly immoral celebrities who wear crosses
- frequent misuse of the holy name of God (aside from blatant profanities using God's name, consider the exclamation "Oh, my God!")
- church sanctuaries used as secular performance halls (perhaps even with an open bar and strobe lighting)
- modern art that juxtaposes Christian symbols with vulgarities and obscenities

To conclude this discussion, you might simply read together Philippians 4:8 and let these words of Scripture sink in as you reflect quietly: "Whatever is true, whatever is noble, whatever is right, whatever is pure, whatever is lovely, whatever is admirable—if anything is excellent or praiseworthy—think about such things."

A Cryptic Message

Although many acts of sacrilege may hardly even be noticed today, there was no denying that God had noticed Belshazzar's act of insolence. As the young ruler and his guests were using the sacred goblets from God's temple to drink their wine and toast their gods, a hand appeared and began writing on the palace wall. Belshazzar was terrified. Maybe he suddenly realized that there might be something to those stories about Nebuchadnezzar after all.

The writing that appeared was in Aramaic, and it seems peculiar that no one could read the inscription. Even though Aramaic was not the native language of the Babylonians, it would seem that with a thousand (presumably educated) nobles present, along with other guests, someone should have been able to decipher the meaning!

This question has puzzled biblical scholars for many years. An interesting possibility appears in a 1639 painting of the scene by Rembrandt van Rijn. The artist portrays the writing as a kind of cryptogram, with the letters written from top to bottom rather than the usual right to left (like Hebrew). Rembrandt was not the first to propose that the words may have appeared in the form of a puzzle, but his depiction clearly shows how it might have confused the Babylonian wise men.

The enchanters, astrologers, and diviners may also have been stumped simply by the meaning of the words. In Aramaic, as noted in the study guide, the words could have a variety of meanings and associations, depending on the vowel points one could apply to the base letters. Since the last word could also be a pun on "Persia," the wise men might have thought the saying could refer to anything from a bill of sale to counting instructions to travel directions!

Attitude and Behavior

Once the wise men had had their turn at trying to interpret the message, our hero, Daniel, was again summoned—this time at the request of the queen mother, who remembered him well (Dan. 5:10-12).

Make sure your group takes note of the attitude with which Daniel responded to the king. Why was it so different from the way he had come before Nebuchadnezzar many years earlier? Take note also of the way in which Daniel told Belshazzar the

Welcome
Psh. 20
prayer

things he already knew about his ancestor, Nebuchadnezzar (5:18-21). Did Belshazzar have any excuse for his behavior?

Do we? What's our reaction to Daniel's statement in 5:23: "But you did not honor the God who holds in his hand your life and all your ways"? Do we show in our lives that we believe this to be true? Do we treat the things of God (including our life and all our ways) in such a way that God is honored?

GENERAL DISCUSSION

1. *Why would Belshazzar order his servants to bring in the gold and silver goblets from the temple in Jerusalem?*

Though we can't be certain of the answer to this question, it's a good one to think about, because it gets at the issue of motivation. Why do we decide to profane holy things? Why do we use God's name in vain when we *know* this dishonors God? In the Ten Commandments God says as clearly as possible that "the LORD will not hold anyone guiltless who misuses his name" (Ex.20:7). Do we suppose God is any less displeased when we misuse sacred things associated with God's holy name?

Though the story in Daniel 5 doesn't provide a clear answer to this question, we can infer a few things from the text. The repeated emphasis on wine in 5:1-4 suggests that Belshazzar was drinking heavily and thus was drunk. Most of us can think of examples of people who made foolish decisions after having too much to drink.

It appears also that Belshazzar was trying to impress his guests. Perhaps, like a hostess setting out the best crystal and silver for special guests, Belshazzar was opening the treasury to bring out the sacred, valuable (and probably beautiful) goblets from Jerusalem. Less clear is whether the king superstitiously believed that these vessels were talismanic, as if he and his guests might receive some benefit or good luck by drinking from them. Since they praised their own gods while drinking from them, it seems more likely that Belshazzar was simply trying to please his own gods by using these vessels.

In connection with this, was the king also thumbing his nose at the God of the Jews? It seems so, at least on the common level of honoring one's own gods over the gods of one's conquered enemies. But from Daniel's statement to the king later, it becomes clearer that Belshazzar may have been deliberately challenging the God of the Jews, whom Nebuchadnezzar had learned to honor (4:34-37). After recounting Nebuchadnezzar's story about being humbled and then restored after acknowledging God, Daniel declares, "But you . . . O Belshazzar, have not humbled yourself, though you knew all this" (5:22-23).

In addition we may wonder if Belshazzar was trying to prove his superiority over his ancestors. In some respects, this may be the most important possibility, because it can help to explain why we also sometimes make foolish choices regarding holy things and practices.

Trying to prove ourselves superior is the exact opposite of demonstrating humility. Like Belshazzar, we may think we are witty or clever to do something sacrilegious, as if we're saying, "I know I can get away with this." Or maybe we fall into the habit of profaning God's name simply because we aren't struck by lightning every time we do it. How often don't we, in one way or another, fail to show humility because we'd rather fit in with everyone else and not be labeled a bore or a prude or "out of it"? (For additional ideas on discussing this topic, see the section "A Young King's Folly" in the preceding leader's notes.)

How foolish! How much greater our joy and blessing can be if we keep everything that belongs to God holy, including our life and all our ways (5:23; also see Mark 7:1-23; 1 Cor. 6:19-20).

2. *Why do you think God sent a hand to write the mysterious message on the wall? For whom was it sent? What did the message accomplish, since Belshazzar's reign was coming to an end that very night?*

Our text says it was "the fingers" of a human hand that wrote on the palace wall (Dan. 5:5). For Jews who would read or hear these words several centuries later, this detail was important. It meant that the writing was from God and that it had the same authority as God's Law. Recall that when Moses was on Mount Sinai, "the two tablets of the Testimony" were "inscribed by the finger of God" (Ex. 31:18). It's worth noting also that Pharaoh's magicians reacted earlier to the plagues by saying, "This is the finger of God" (8:19).

So one group that benefited from God's writing on the wall was Jewish people in the second century B.C. who were living under persecution and needed to know that their cruel oppressor (Antiochus IV Epiphanes) would be found wanting, just as Belshazzar had been. For them, the vision of God's fingers wrote a message of assurance on the palace wall.

The thousand nobles who were gathered for Belshazzar's feast also benefited from seeing God's writing on the wall. We can imagine how news of this incident would quickly spread, and how people would likely show respect for anything related to the God of the Jews—maybe even the Jews themselves—when they heard about what happened to Belshazzar.

Belshazzar himself also benefited, if only briefly. How often don't we want to know why things happen the way they do? If Belshazzar had been challenging God, he surely knew now that God was real. And he now had no reason for doubt or confusion about his fate; Daniel told him exactly why the kingdom was being divided.

Through the words of Daniel, God's writing on the wall continues to accomplish God's purposes. Though "the handwriting on the wall" has become a common saying, its origin is waiting in Daniel 5 for anyone who wants to learn more about it. The lesson is clear—God desires us to honor the holy name of God and to keep things associated with God's name holy. Obedience to this aspect of God's will is a sign of our humility, which is pleasing to God.

3. *If Daniel was a teenager when taken into exile, he may well have been more than eighty years old at the time of these events. Would that have made a difference in the way he responded to the king? Explain.*

If there are older adults in your group, invite them to talk a little about how they are different now than when they were in their teens and twenties. How do our attitudes change as we mature and gain wisdom?

One thing that changes is our experience. The longer we live, the more we learn—if we are paying attention to the things God is trying to teach us throughout our lives. Daniel learned from his experience with the royal food at the king's table; he learned from interpreting Nebuchadnezzar's dreams; he learned from his friends' experience in the fiery furnace. Everything taught him that God was faithful. God would not abandon him or his friends simply because they were in exile.

Of course, there are always some adults who seem bound and determined not to learn. Not surprisingly, we often describe their behavior as immature.

Another thing that changes as we age is that we learn to value people for who they are, not for what they own, who they know, or what work they do. More than any other age group (except maybe infants and small children), seniors appreciate the value of relationships more than material things and the worldly status that goes with them. As one of my former pastors said when he was asked why he and his wife chose to have seven children, "What joy will owning more things give me when I've become an old man?"

Daniel almost seems disgusted with Belshazzar and with how little he seemed to know about relationships. The king was trying to impress his guests with goblets from the temple of Jerusalem, but what lasting value would that bring? Daniel knew that being a faithful friend, leading with integrity, and being an honest servant were far better ways to win people's lasting favor and respect.

Most important, the passing of years teaches us how much we can trust God. Just as Daniel knew he no longer needed to fear what the Babylonians might do to him, so we can be confident—at any age—that God is with us and will never leave us or forsake us (Matt. 28:20; Heb. 13:5-6).

4. *Daniel reminded Belshazzar of what had happened to his ancestor Nebuchadnezzar. How can the stories of people who have gone before us help us learn to trust in God?*

If Belshazzar truly believed the stories of what had happened to Nebuchadnezzar, there's no accounting for his foolishness in drinking from the sacred vessels of the God of the Jews. He was just daring God to put him in his place. Even (more likely) if he knew the stories well but disregarded them, it seems clear that his using the goblets to toast other gods (Dan. 5:3-4) was a direct challenge to the God of the Jews.

Unfortunately that same assessment can be made of many people today who know the stories of the Bible, who believe they are true, and who still choose to live as if God doesn't really mean what God says. Thankfully the Lord is a God of grace and mercy: God "does not treat us as our sins deserve or repay us according to our iniquities" (Ps. 103:10). We are given time to learn from people who've gone before us, to humble ourselves before God, to confess our sins, to receive God's grace, and to live thankfully for the gift of new life God gives in Christ.

Often it is the stories of faithful ancestors that encourage people who do not know the Word to turn to God's Word, where they can find even more stories about faithful people in the family of God. As believers in Christ, we are called to share our own stories with family members and neighbors and to help nurture them as they "grow in the grace and knowledge of our Lord and Savior Jesus Christ" (2 Pet. 3:18).

The benefit for all of us who hear stories of faith is that we can learn from the mistakes others have made. In many ways, and always by the power of the Spirit working in us, we ought to be able to avoid the trouble experienced by those, like Belshazzar, who refuse to listen and thus learn the hard way.

Any story that can help someone come to faith in Jesus is a story worth telling. Whether it's a story from the Bible or from our own experience, if it leads to faith, it's a gift from God, a gift to be shared often.

5. *Why couldn't the king's wise men figure out the meaning of the message on the wall? How did the words of the inscription spell out Belshazzar's fate? Do you think he doubted the accuracy of Daniel's interpretation?*

Along with comments in the study guide and in the preceding leader's notes about the meaning of the inscription, you may want to discuss the monetary units in terms that are familiar to everyone. For example, what would we think of an inscription that read, "Fifty cents, a penny, a quarter"? When we think of the message in these terms, we can see how it might be puzzling to Belshazzar's "enchanters, astrologers and diviners" (Dan. 5:7)—and perhaps even more so if they didn't catch the connection to the misuse of objects that were holy to the Lord.

The secondary meaning of the words, having to do with weights (monetary units were calculated by weight in those days), completed the puzzle: numbered, weighed, divided. Daniel explained that Belshazzar's days were numbered; that he had been weighed on the scales and found wanting (like the relationship between a mina and a shekel), and that his kingdom would be divided (or halved) between the Medes and Persians.

You could also note that other solutions to the riddle of this inscription have been suggested. One interesting one proposes that *mene* refers to Nebuchadnezzar, that the much smaller *tekel* refers to his son Evil-Merodach (or perhaps to Nabonidus, Belshazzar's father), and that *parsin* refers to Belshazzar, whose kingdom was about to be divided.

Whichever meaning we accept for each of the individual words in the message, emphasize that Daniel saw the ultimate meaning of the full inscription and spelled it out for Belshazzar. It's hard to imagine that the king doubted Daniel's interpretation, but whether he believed it or not, he immediately gave the prophet the promised reward, just as Nebuchadnezzar had rewarded Daniel for his wisdom in the past (see 2:46-49). What's more, Belshazzar didn't have to wait long to see if Daniel's interpretation was correct, for "that very night" he lost his life and his kingdom was over-taken (5:30-31).

For additional discussion: If even a corrupt and sacrilegious king like Belshazzar believed Daniel, why do so many people today hesitate to believe God's Word? Isn't the truth of it self-evident?

SMALL GROUP SESSION IDEAS

Opening (10 minutes)

Once everyone has gathered, ask if anyone tried the optional study project from session 4 about writing a song in the style of Hannah or Mary or paraphrasing one of those songs into modern words. If so, invite people to share their work with the group.

Transition into your study of Daniel 5 by asking if anyone has ever "profaned" something considered holy, either at home or in the church (playing in the baptismal font, rolling communion bread into little balls, and so on). Ask how they felt about it then, and what they think about it now. Why is it important to set some things apart as sacred?

Prayer—Begin by reading Psalm 20. Thank God for sacred things and practices, reflecting on some of them specifically. Ask God to make this study session a time that's set apart to honor the Lord our God.

Share—This session reinforces some of the lessons about pride that surfaced in the previous session. As a group, make a list of words you could use to describe a proud person; then make a list of words to describe a humble person (if possible, write the lists on a chalkboard or newsprint). Reflect quietly and honestly on which traits describe you.

Focus—If the last session could be summarized by *hubris* (overweening pride), this one centers on *sacrilege* (prideful desecration of sacred things). Keep these questions in mind during this session: *What has God set apart as holy in my life, and why? How do I honor God when I keep those things holy?*

Growing (35-40 minutes)

Read—To read Daniel 5 together in your group, you may choose to have several people read the various parts out loud: narrator, Belshazzar, the queen, and Daniel.

Study Guide??

Discuss—Use the following questions to expand on the questions listed under General Discussion. Several of these look at the situation in Daniel 5 from a broader perspective.

- Though his age is not stated, we can be fairly certain that Belshazzar was a young man (his father, Nabonidus, was still living). How does our appreciation for sacred things change with age? What kinds of events occur in our lives to correct the impetuous and sometimes foolish decisions we make when we're young?

- If you could recommend that God send a hand to write on someone's wall today, whose wall would it be, and why? What would the message say? What might a message on your own wall say?

- Daniel paid no attention to the king's promised reward for discerning the message. How much do we allow the prospect of some benefit to affect the way we deal with God's Word? For example, how would we deal with a situation that might help us financially but that we also knew was against God's Word?

- Daniel's faith was unhesitating in this story. What are some ways in which we can become more secure in our faith?

Goalsetting (5 minutes)
Set a goal to take note of short, public slogans "written on the wall" all around us. For example, a shoe company says "Just do it"; a soda company claims that its product is "the real thing." Bumper stickers are another source of public sentiments. In general, what do these messages encourage us to do? How many (proportionally) go against God's will for us?

Closing (10 minutes)
Preparing for Prayer—Ask group members to think of three- or four-word prayer requests, as brief (and yet profound) as God's message for the king. Share these, perhaps writing them down. Make them the foundation of your closing prayer.

Prayer—Read Psalm 20:6-8 again. Acknowledge the holiness of God, and ask for the strength to keep sacred things holy. Invite everyone also to include the prayer requests they've shared.

Group Study Project (Optional)
In addition to the Goalsetting suggestion, group members may wish to keep an eye out for other examples of sacrilege in our society. Where and when are sacred things that are devoted to God profaned?

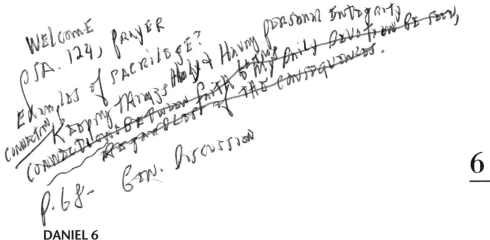

6

DANIEL 6

Into the Lions' Den

In a Nutshell

A martyr story, a miracle story, a prophecy of the resurrection—all have been suggested as legitimate ways to read the story about Daniel in the lions' den. In this final narrative in the book of Daniel, we find our hero, a servant of God, set against the servants of Darius the king, and we find God's law set against the irrevocable law of the Medes and Persians. This story, with its theme of deliverance, serves as a fitting transition to Daniel's prophecies in chapters 7-12 pointing to the complete future deliverance of God's people.

More Than Meets the Eye

As with several of the other familiar stories in Daniel, it's possible to read this story too quickly. Part of your job as leader is to encourage group members to look for and savor the story's details. Again we have before us an elegant narrative prepared by one of the Bible's master storytellers.

Group members may notice several themes emerging as the lesson progresses. Some of the themes people might identify are

- envy and its consequences.
- law-keeping versus law-breaking.
- public displays of faithfulness.
- the pain of regret.
- the mercy and power of God.
- the fate of the wicked.
- the praise of God.

In addition this story also contains many parallels with the death and resurrection story of Jesus, as noted in the study guide.

Another introductory detail that you may want to discuss with your group is that Daniel was a very old man at the time

DANIEL: DARING FAITH IN DANGEROUS TIMES

these events took place, probably in his mid- to late eighties. Consider asking some questions like these: *Does this surprise anyone? How does this fact affect our understanding of the story? In light of this detail, why would so many children's Bible story books choose to depict Daniel as a young man in this story? Have we been overlooking an important lesson about the faith of older adults?*

Obeying a Higher Law

Daniel, fully aware of the king's decree (6:10), went home and deliberately violated the new law. Just as he had always done, he knelt toward Jerusalem before his open window and gave thanks to God. Daniel neither flaunted his practice nor made an effort to conceal it. He simply continued doing what he had always done.

Is this good advice for someone who finds himself or herself in a situation in which worship seems either uncomfortable or perhaps even illegal? If, for example, the issue is a young person who has always prayed kneeling by his bed, and now he's wondering if he should still do this at college with a new roommate watching, it would probably be sound advice to say, "Sure, keep on doing what you've been doing." But if the situation involves a new convert to Christianity in a country where conversion is prohibited, should that person be encouraged to endanger his or her life and possibly the lives of other family members?

These are difficult questions. Christians have always struggled with the need to obey the laws of the lands in which they live (which seems to be the counsel of Rom. 13:1-7), and yet they must also obey the higher law of God's Word. For example, if a country issues a law that says that you must kill all people of a certain race, God's law is clearly more important, and must be obeyed. If, on the other hand, the secular law is clearly benign—no jaywalking, for example—and violates no part of God's Word, Christians should set a good example and obey the law.

King Darius's new decree outlawed the worship of God. In this case, Daniel decided that God's higher law regarding prayer and worship had to take precedence.

Truth and Consequences

Once the king had been tricked into making a new law and confirming it, he was powerless to revoke his own decree (Dan. 6:12-14). It can often happen that we also follow a thoughtless course of action that cannot be reversed. Sexual activity is one example, spreading rumors or lies about someone is another. In these and many other situations, once damage is done, it cannot be undone. As a result, believers must always practice integrity, thinking carefully about the consequences of all their actions.

Although the king tried to find a way to spare Daniel, he was eventually forced to abide by his own decree. Darius ordered Daniel thrown into the pit, but he also offered his hope that Daniel's God would rescue him (6:16).

As leader, you may wish to note that people often want to find rational explanations for miracles portrayed in the Bible. In this situation, they may want to suggest that the king fed the lions generously before abiding by his new law and throwing Daniel into the pit. But nothing of the sort is even hinted at in the text; we are clearly intended to see the outcome as a miracle. Besides, if the lions' bellies were full, what would account for their voracity when Daniel's enemies were thrown in?

When the king returned in the morning and Daniel explained that God's angel had shut the lions' mouths, Daniel added, "They have not hurt me, because I was found innocent in [God's] sight. Nor have I ever done any wrong before you, O king" (6:22). Note the point Daniel was making here: he had wronged neither God nor Darius—even though he had deliberately violated the king's new decree! In other words, the flaw was in the decree itself, not in Daniel's decision to ignore it.

The king didn't need much convincing; he now knew that his other administrators had tried to deceive him. So he ordered them—and their families, in accord with ancient Persian custom—thrown into the lions' den, where they were promptly devoured.

A New Decree

This first half of Daniel concludes with a new law of the Medes and Persians, presumably as irrevocable as the decree that was supposed to end Daniel's life. This time the people were ordered to "fear and reverence the God of Daniel" (6:26). As noted in the study guide, Darius's words of praise foreshadow prophecies about God's eternal kingdom that are recorded in the remaining chapters of the book.

Having come to the end of the most familiar part of Daniel, your challenge as leader will be to build and sustain interest for the remaining three lessons, which cover the remaining six chapters of the book. You may want to issue a decree of your own—that anyone who has studied this far in Daniel must also finish this study and see Daniel through to the end. Make it irrevocable!

GENERAL DISCUSSION

1. In what ways does this chapter testify to Daniel's professional integrity? His personal integrity? To what extent should the two be related in a person's life?

Over the past few decades, people in the United States have had the unfortunate experience of seeing a series of leaders in politics, business, and religion come under scrutiny for their integrity—or lack of it. All too often, some questionable activities have been uncovered. While not every one of those leaders was found guilty of breaking the law, many cases involved the appearance of impropriety and questionable ethics.

The result? A lack of trust in people who hold leadership positions and make decisions that affect many other people. Perhaps unfairly, many of us also assume that an accusation is as good as a conviction because we've seen the old saying confirmed too many times: Where there's smoke, there's fire.

Such was not the case with Daniel. The prophet was a man of extraordinary integrity, both professional and personal. When his enemies scrutinized his professional service to the king, they could find no flaw. When they examined his personal life, they realized that the only way they could attack his integrity was to somehow discredit him for his devotion to God.

Daniel's demonstrations of professional and personal integrity are very clear in this story—and so are the consequences, as well as God's triumph over wrong. What is less clear for us is the way in which professional and personal integrity should be related in our lives today. Should there be one kind of ethics for our personal lives, and another for business or politics? Should there be one standard of integrity for our relationship with God and another for our relationships with people? Should there be different standards of behavior depending on whether an activity is public or private?

The hard but truthful answer is no—even though we don't always live that way. There shouldn't be different ethics, different kinds of integrity, or different standards of behavior depending on whether something is personal or professional.

Public figures (politics, business, religion) under scrutiny for their integrity or lack of.

We should always live according to the highest standards, whether a million people are watching or only God is watching us. That's the standard Daniel followed in Babylon. *EX: p. 66*

What's more common today is rationalization for engaging in questionable ethics. For example, suppose Daniel had cut a few corners in his administrative work—who would have criticized him? After all, he was an exile, a prisoner of war. Would it have been so wrong to take advantage of the situation for a little personal gain? That kind of rationalization is all too common today:

- "Everyone does it, so why shouldn't I?"
- "This is a big company; they'll never notice if I take a little something for myself."
- "All my predecessors in office did it; I was just following their example."

Invite group members to add some rationalizations of their own.

It can be so easy to let our integrity slip, and the consequences might seem very minor. But the lesson we can learn from Daniel is that integrity does matter—both in our personal and professional lives. We show gratitude for God's faithfulness when we honor God in every part of our lives.

2. *The laws of the Medes and Persians could not "be repealed" (Dan. 6:8). Is this a good idea? What effect would this have on the writing of new laws today?*

At first glance, we might say this is not such a good idea (and under our democratic systems of government, it would probably be unworkable). There is not even much documentary evidence outside of the Bible to show that this was the long-term policy of the Medo-Persian Empire. This question can be thought-provoking, though, because it gets at the purpose and necessity of laws.

God's laws are irrevocable, as Jesus made clear in the Sermon on the Mount: "Do not think that I have come to abolish the Law or the Prophets; I have not come to abolish them but to fulfill them. I tell you the truth, until heaven and earth disappear, not the smallest letter, not the least stroke of a pen, will by any means disappear from the Law until everything is accomplished" (Matt. 5:17-18). God's laws are permanent because they teach us our sin, encourage us to recognize our need for a Savior, and restrain our behavior.

69

Should human laws be equally irrevocable? Probably not, since we are not perfect and even our best laws contain flaws. Should we then pass lots of laws and endlessly modify, repeal, or reinstitute them as necessary to fit new situations? Sad to say, this may be our best course of action. This approach can be complicated and costly, but the past few centuries of Western history show that we haven't come up with a better way.

If everyone's behavior were marked by integrity like Daniel's, we wouldn't need many laws, and we could probably pass a few that were irrevocable; we might not need much more than the Ten Commandments. On the other hand, wherever personal integrity is lacking, more laws are needed to restrain behavior, and we might want those laws to be easily modified in order to keep up with the latest in unethical behavior.

The necessity of new laws and the frequency with which they are passed reminds us how far our society is from behavior that's as trustworthy as Daniel's. With every new law we're reminded that we have a long way to go in learning to live by faith.

3. *Was Daniel breaking the law when he prayed toward Jerusalem? Whose law? When he was released from the lions' den, he told the king that he had done no wrong before him. What did Daniel mean by that? Should Christians disregard laws they do not agree with? Explain.*

Strictly speaking, Daniel broke King Darius's new law when he continued praying to God as he had always done. But he was also correct to tell the king that he had done no wrong before him. Daniel's decision to honor God took nothing away from his faithful service to the king.

Christians have long had to decide what to do when human laws are in conflict with God's law. The example given in the preceding leader's notes is an easy one. If a nation passed a law saying that all people of a certain race were to be killed, any believer could violate that law in good conscience, knowing that it's more important to obey God's commands "You shall not murder" (Ex. 20:13) and "Love one another" (John 13:34; see also Matt. 22:36-40).

In the same way, if a government passed a law that said it was illegal to worship any God other than the one designated by the government, a believer could confidently break that law and continue to praise God. This is essentially what happened in Daniel's case. It also happens today in many countries around the world in which it's illegal to worship God or practice Christianity.

The question becomes more difficult when we have to deal with laws that are not so clearly against God's Word. For example, should Christians serve in the military, knowing that they might be called on to kill other human beings? Should believers pay taxes that are used to pay for weapons of war? Should Christians abide by laws that prevent them from witnessing to women who are on their way to abortion clinics? In many of these cases, there is no simple right or wrong answer, and believers will have to search their consciences, consult the wisdom of the Christian community, listen for God's Spirit, and make their decision.

What Christians should *not* do is assume that human laws are of little or no consequence, to be ignored whenever they are inconvenient (as in the case of speed limits, for example). The apostle Paul made clear that human governments and the laws they pass have a legitimate place in God's plan, and that we should honor God by honoring the people God has placed in positions of authority (Rom. 13:1-7).

4. *In this story, which of the parallels with Jesus' death and resurrection strikes you most powerfully?*   P 39, STUDY GUIDE

Each person in the group should be free to decide which of the parallels they find most compelling. If there's time, encourage everyone to participate in answering this question. Mention that it can be interesting to find out which details strike each person and why—and that we can often gain new insights from each other's perspectives.

For me, the most striking detail is the deliberate act of sealing Daniel into the lions' den. King Darius seals the stone "with his own signet ring and with the rings of his nobles" so that everyone in authority was both a witness and an underwriter of Daniel's sentence. In other words, his fate was sealed, as far as Babylon's government was concerned. Similarly, Matthew records that Jesus' dead body was sealed in its tomb: "They went and made the tomb secure by putting a seal on the stone and posting the guard" (Matt. 27:66). These seals serve God's purpose of assuring us that a miracle really did take place, both in the lions' den and in the Savior's tomb.

5. *How does God's law triumph over human law in this story?*

The most obvious triumph of God's law in this story occurs when Daniel survives unscathed from his ordeal in the lions' den. But a less obvious triumph had already occurred in Daniel's heart, as displayed by his actions. He continued to honor God in worship and prayer even though Darius had decreed otherwise. When Daniel was found guilty of failing to obey the king's human-made, human-worshiping law, he was thrown to the lions. If he hadn't survived, that wouldn't have meant God couldn't save him, as Daniel's three friends had earlier confessed (Dan. 3:17-18). And when Daniel survived, it was simply clearer that God's law had won.

Along with the other stories we've studied so far in the book of Daniel, this entire incident demonstrates the superiority of faith in God as a way of life. Daniel gave no heed to what would have been the "smart" thing to do. He didn't eat King Nebuchadnezzar's food; he didn't soften his interpretation of the king's dreams; he didn't hesitate to read the writing on the wall; and he didn't bow down and worship King Darius. Again and again, Daniel demonstrated the superiority of living by faith in God—which includes obeying God's laws.

Obedience is still important today, when so many people often choose to do the "smart" thing and follow the way of the world. We need to lift up the example of Daniel again and again, because he so clearly demonstrates the superior wisdom of living by faith in God.

SMALL GROUP SESSION IDEAS

Opening (10 minutes)

In the Goalsetting section near the end of session 5, we noted that short statements like ad slogans and bumper stickers often encourage us to act or think a certain way. As people arrive, invite them to write some of these on a marker board or poster sheet you've hung on the wall, using different colored markers and writing styles for emphasis, if they like. How many of the slogans or phrases go against what we believe as Christians? Spend a few moments discussing the effect of living in a society that bombards us with these kinds of messages.

Prayer—As the group begins to think about maintaining personal integrity in the midst of non-Christian influences, read Psalm 124, which reminds us that we cannot stand up in our own strength against God's enemies. Thank God for always being with those who have faith in the Lord, and ask the Holy Spirit to use this study time as a tool to build your courage.

Share—Ask if any group members observed examples of sacrilege since the last session. If so, how did they react to it? Take a moment also to think about a connection between keeping things holy and having personal integrity. Remember Paul's words: "Don't you know that you yourselves are God's temple and that God's Spirit lives in you?" (1 Cor. 3:16).

Focus—Personal integrity is the key concept in this lesson. When Daniel, the flawless administrator, is forced to decide between continuing his practice of daily prayer or obeying the king's capricious new decree, he chooses to continue his commitment to God. Keep these questions in mind throughout the rest of this session: *What is the connection between my faith and my daily devotion to God? Do I hide it, or do I let my devotion show, regardless of the consequences?*

Growing (35-40 minutes)

Read—Again consider having one person read the Scripture for this lesson while others listen. You may also want to read or review portions of the notes in the study guide or leader's guide.

Discuss—The following questions are designed to help everyone bridge the gap between ancient Medo-Persia and the world of today. Use these questions wherever they fit best as you do the General Discussion questions.

- If you rated your personal integrity on a scale of 1 to 10, with 1 being low and 10 being perfect, what score would you give yourself? Would others give you a higher or lower score? Explain.

- What evidence in your life and actions could prove to others that you are a Christian?

- If you were traveling in a foreign country known to be hostile toward Christians, in what ways, if any, would your behavior change?

- King Darius felt trapped after his ego allowed him to be duped. When has your ego gotten you into trouble?

- How does trusting in God "shut the mouths of the lions"? Does living by faith mean we will never be wounded, physically or spiritually? Would the point of this story be any different if Daniel had been devoured by the lions?

Goalsetting (5 minutes)

Between this session and the next, look for different ways in which faith is revealed, both in your life and in the lives of others around you. Also make it a goal to thank someone—in person or by letter, phone, or e-mail—for letting his or her faith show. Be prepared to share about this experience at your next group meeting.

Closing (10 minutes)

Preparing for Prayer—The personal integrity of people who follow Jesus is critical to the way others perceive Christianity. Before praying, invite members of the group to spend a few moments in silence, thinking about areas of personal integrity in which they need strengthening from God. Group members may mention other concerns and praises as well.

Prayer—Begin your closing prayer time by reading Darius's decree in Daniel 6:26-27, changing the pronouns from third person to second person ("he" to "you"). Continue by thanking God for amazing signs and wonders in the life of Daniel and for rescuing us through Jesus Christ. Allow a few moments of silence for everyone to talk with God about matters of integrity (either silently or aloud) and to mention other items. Then end your prayer for this session with a reading of Psalm 138.

Study Project (Optional)

The remaining chapters of Daniel are often referred to as *apocalyptic literature.* Invite members of the group to look up this term in a Bible dictionary or encyclopedia before your next study session. Also ask if anyone would be willing to make a brief presentation on apocalyptic literature at the beginning of the next session.

7

DANIEL 7-8

Beastly Visions

In a Nutshell

As we move into the second half of the book of Daniel, we encounter two visions about strange beasts. These visions reveal the unfolding course of events in both Daniel's era and in the future. What's more, the Bible's interpretation of the visions assures us not only of God's control over history but also of the ultimate victory of the Lord's eternal kingdom.

A Change of Literary Styles

Do you like reading westerns? What about romance novels? Maybe you're a science fiction fan. Or perhaps a good murder mystery really grabs your attention. Each of these are different genres of fiction, and they are easily identified by their unique characteristics.

Ask group members about their taste in fiction and then take them back to the example of the western—a type of fiction that isn't finding much of an audience these days. It's entirely possible that westerns will fade from the literary scene before long as the genre's most avid readers also "ride off into the sunset."

Many of us still understand the literary conventions included in many westerns and popularized by TV shows and movies like *Gunsmoke* and *Wild, Wild West.* There's always the fight scene in the tavern in which the mirror over the bar or piano gets smashed and someone gets thrown out through the swinging front doors. There's also the shootout on the dusty main street (complete with rolling tumbleweed), black hats for bad guys and white hats for good guys, the hard-living barmaid with the heart of gold, and more. As soon as we notice any of these elements, we know just what we're reading or watching, and we have a pretty good sense of what's going to happen next. We even anticipate it because it's an expected part of the genre.

Now, imagine a reader a few hundred years from now stumbling across a long-forgotten western novel. What would that person make of this type of literature? Would the imagery make sense? If the person read the term "ten gallon hat" or found a reference to the "OK Corral" without any further explanation, would he or she have any idea what they meant? Probably not.

That's the kind of problem we often encounter with apocalyptic literature, a genre that was most popular from about 200 B.C. to A.D. 300. Apocalyptic literature deals with the ultimate triumph of good over evil, especially at the end of time. Characteristics of the genre include heavenly messengers, strange beasts, rapidly changing visions, battles on earth and in heaven, and, of course, the final victory of good. We find all of these elements in the second half of the book of Daniel.

Since we rarely read this type of literature anymore (and probably understand it even less), we tend to be wary of it. We tend to imbue it with more mystery than was ever intended, and many people even regard it superstitiously, believing that if they just knew the secret code, this literature would reveal everything they would want to know about the future.

But these writings contain no secret code, no detailed, hidden map of the future—only what God has chosen to reveal, in plain view. The primary purpose of apocalyptic prose is not so much to predict the future as it is to comfort future generations of believers. Apocalyptic writings continue to reassure us that God is in control and that everything is unfolding according to God's plan.

Beasts and Interpretations

As the leader, your hardest task during the next few sessions may be to help your group members let go of any preconceived notions they have about unlocking mysteries in apocalyptic literature. If anyone comes to you and offers to explain how "this beast represents the United States" and "that beast represents China," run away screaming in the other direction as fast as possible. There's no reason to believe that our generation has been singled out for special revelation through these verses. Point out that the Bible speaks to God's people in *every* generation.

Daniel's heavenly visitors do a good job of helping us keep our feet on the ground and our head out of the clouds. Their primary message is this: there's a lot of history coming, and some of it may be unpleasant—but it's all under God's control.

What's truly wonderful about the visions in Daniel 7-8 is that God sent interpreters to explain their meanings. Make sure you reinforce the concept that Scripture is its own best interpreter, perhaps especially with apocalyptic texts—and use these chapters as an example. The angelic messengers don't tell us everything about every detail, but they tell us enough; it's our responsibility to avoid indulging in fanciful speculations about the rest.

It's Under Control

Perhaps the most important lesson in these two chapters of Daniel is that God has it all under control. Nothing is happening apart from the Lord's will. God knows all about the rise and fall of empires. God knows all about big horns and little horns. God knows that faithful believers will be under tremendous pressure. God also knows that in the end the kingdom of righteousness will be established forever.

Read the final judgment scene again in Daniel 7:9-10. What do you suppose is written in those books? Revelation 20:12 says, "The dead were judged according to what they had done as recorded in the books." God knows that things sometimes seem unfair to us, but our Lord has it all under control. It's all being recorded, and at the final judgment God will set everything right.

GENERAL DISCUSSION

1. *Instead of sending Daniel visions of a lion, a bear, a leopard, a ten-horned beast, a ram, and a goat, why didn't God just tell him plainly about the Medes, Persians, Greeks, and so on? What purposes might the animal symbols serve?*

We could ask this same question about any apocalyptic text in the Bible. Why must they be so obscure? Why can't the names, dates, and places simply be identified in plain terms? People have proposed many answers to this sort of question, but probably the best answer is that it all has to do with faith.

Imagine for a moment that we were living near the time of Christ's return and that the book of Revelation said there would one day be a nation called the United States of America that would dominate the world. Imagine too that the enemies of the United States were spelled out equally clearly, and that a specific date for a final battle and judgment were identified. Knowing so many details, along with knowing that God would make no mistake in revealing them, where would be the need for faith? People would read Revelation, observe history unfolding exactly as described, and they would either choose to be on the side of God or the side of evil—but then they'd also know that evil was going to lose, so why choose that side? What's more, because people would know the date of the end, there'd be no reason to encourage others to follow Jesus.

In short, if God had written out the future in year-by-year detail, we might question the need to live by faith. Make sure your group takes a few moments to think through and discuss this matter.

Instead of describing the future in specific detail, God has given us a description of the *kinds* of things that must take place before the end of time comes—and they may take place more than once for more than one group of people. In this way, visions like the ones we've been examining in Daniel can speak to people anywhere at any time in history, and they can encourage God's people to live by faith, knowing that God is firmly in control.

This perspective helps to explain the use of animal metaphors too. Yes, the bear in Daniel 7 likely refers to the Medo-Persian alliance, and the indescribable beast probably represents Rome. But couldn't we also say that in the twentieth century Nazi Germany was like a bear with bones in its teeth, or that the Soviet Union was like a beast with many horns? Couldn't Hitler or Stalin be perceived as examples of the boastful horn that was slain (Dan. 7:11)? Or what about Mao Zedong, Pol Pot, Ferdinand Marcos, or, more recently, Saddam Hussein?

The animal metaphors not only help us apply the truth of these visions to different times; they also identify the characteristics of rulers and nations that choose to rely on their own power and resources rather than placing their trust in God.

Never forget that we are created to be better than beasts, to have dominion over the beasts. When we choose to live like animals, we deny our own uniqueness in God's creation, and we become little more than dumb brutes. It's far better to "raise [our] eyes toward heaven," as Nebuchadnezzar learned (Dan. 4:34), and to look to God for strength.

2. *What relationship is there between the stories of faith in the first half of Daniel and the beastly visions in Daniel 7-8? What role does faith play in the vision accounts?*

In each of the stories in the first half of Daniel, we find individual heroes—Daniel and his three companions—who are faced with a decision about living by faith. Daniel could have ignored God's dietary laws and eaten the king's royal food, but he chose to live by faith, eating only vegetables and drinking only water. Shadrach, Meshach, and Abednego could have bowed down to the king's statue along with everyone else, but they chose to live by faith, even when threatened with death in a blazing furnace. Daniel could have stopped praying to God for thirty days, but he chose to continue his worship of God and to face a den of lions. Each of these stories is about the triumph of faith by God's strength and power. Not surprisingly, so are the stories about Nebuchadnezzar's dreams and about the writing on the wall.

Similarly, the vision accounts in the second half of Daniel are about faith. But in these accounts it isn't a single person or a few individuals who must choose to remain faithful to God; it's an entire people. As empires rise and fall, as battles are waged and the people of God are persecuted, they are challenged to remain faithful, to trust in God for the promised victory in the end for all of God's people. At this point the book of Daniel expands on the individual challenge of living by faith—each person choosing to follow God in a given situation—to encourage the people of God as a group to live by faith.

This movement from individual faith to the faith of an entire people is an important reminder in our culture, in which our faith tends to be very individualistic. A common attitude today implies that each person is responsible for his or her own faith; faith is commonly understood as an individual, even private, choice. As a result, many people in our culture recoil at the idea of *persuading* other people to live by faith and urging them to become part of the family of God.

While there certainly is a personal, individual aspect to having faith in God, living by faith was never meant to be an individual pursuit. God has always called his people together as a body of believers. The New Testament makes especially clear that we are united as the body of Christ, which gives us responsibility for each other's attitudes, behaviors, and spiritual nurture (1 Cor. 12:12-27; Eph. 4:11-16).

The unfolding visions in the second half of Daniel encourage God's people to remain strong in faith together, to encourage one another as they await the "one like a son of man" (Dan. 7:13), the "Prince of princes" (8:25).

3. *Try to picture yourself as a Jew living under persecution sometime after the return from exile (538 B.C.) and before the coming of*

Christ. How do you think you would have reacted to these vision stories in the book of Daniel? Would you have believed what they said about the end of persecution and the restoration of the temple? Why or why not?

It can be hard to imagine ourselves living as persecuted Jews in the intertestamentary period. Palestine was a battleground on countless occasions after the time of the Babylonian captivity and the release of the Jewish exiles. After the Medes and Persians and the Greeks came the Ptolemies and the Seleucids. And then, of course, came Rome. To help us put this in perspective, all this rising and falling of kingdom after kingdom and persecution after persecution had been going on for more than twice as long as either the United States or Canada has been a nation! As someone living in that region back then, it would have been difficult to believe that God was really in control—it may often have seemed that life was only random and cruel.

Yet here was the book of Daniel's prophecies, and, amazingly, the prophet had seen it all coming. Hundreds of years earlier, God had given Daniel visions about many things that would take place, and history was following God's script. In many ways that would have been reassuring to know.

Would we have believed it? That's something individuals must answer for themselves. The accuracy of what Daniel was shown would have been a strong argument in favor of trusting his prophecies. In addition, God's Word offered hope, and hope was sorely needed under the worst of Antiochus's and other rulers' persecutions.

What might have been hardest to believe was how swiftly the situation could change from bitter persecution to freedom from persecution. For example, after only about three-and-a-half years of desecration and persecution by Antiochus IV, the Jews were freed and able to rededicate the temple. Could anyone have guessed that someone as blatantly cruel as Antiochus would fade from power so quickly?

The question remains whether we believe the continuing promise of hope offered in God's Word for all who put their faith in Jesus. Do we truly believe that Christ will return and restore all things that have been desecrated by sin? Do we watch for signs of Christ's return while also striving to serve faithfully, knowing that "only the Father" knows the day or hour when Christ will come again (Matt. 24:36)?

4. *Antiochus was a type of antichrist living before Christ was even born. Who are some of the people most strongly opposed to the*

reign of Christ today? How do they oppress believers? What do Daniel's visions say about the destiny of such oppressors?

In every generation enemies of God have attempted to suppress worship, eliminate (or amend) God's Word, and destroy faith in God. To accomplish these things, people have used every method at their disposal—military campaigns, political power, claims of heavenly visions, economic persuasion, threats to personal safety, and more. These enemies of God have ranged from evil megalomaniacs to sorely misguided idealists. And while some have been easy to recognize, others have managed to delude millions before their true agendas became known. Identifying such people requires vigilance; they can often appear reasonable, and their words can sound appealing.

We need to test first of all whether their message is consistent with God's Word. Are they teaching something contrary to Scripture? For example, do they say God cares only about one particular group of people? That would be a warning sign. Do they place themselves or their needs ahead of others? Are they obsessed with money or power? Do their words match their deeds? Do they humble themselves before God, or do they expect others to humble themselves in their presence?

The ways in which antichrists oppress believers in Christ are as numerous as there are oppressors. Some attempt to crush believers through cruelty and threats. Others promise prosperity or earthly bliss or some kind of special salvation. Perhaps most insidious is the kind of oppression that sounds like the Christian faith but ultimately denies the one way to salvation through Jesus Christ (John 14:6).

As believers, we can take comfort in knowing that ultimately such oppressors cannot stand against the power of God; indeed, no one can snatch God's people from the Father's hand (John 10:27-29). As both of the visions in Daniel 7-8 indicate, anyone who oppresses God's people will eventually be "destroyed" (7:26; 8:25). And in the end "the sovereignty, power and greatness of the kingdoms under the whole heaven will be handed over to the saints, the people of the Most High. His kingdom will be an everlasting kingdom, and all rulers will worship and obey him" (7:27).

5. *How can we use these prophecies in God's Word to encourage believers and strengthen faith today?*

I like to do magic tricks, especially card tricks. I'm a bad magician, though, because I love to tell people how each trick is done. I lay it out step by step, and by the time I'm done explaining, people are often saying, "Let me try it." They want to learn the trick and pass it along to others.

That's the way I feel about these chapters in Daniel. I want to lay out what Daniel is teaching, verse by verse, to show that there's nothing terribly mysterious there, nothing so hard to understand that we can't grasp at least some of it. It's also helpful to remember that God intends for these passages to comfort and assure us, to let us know that the Lord is fully in control of what's going on and will bring it all to a good and glorious end.

Through greater knowledge of God's Word comes greater faith. Showing others that these prophecies have come true—and are still being fulfilled in various ways—can be a great encouragement to believers to stand strong in the faith of the one true Lord and God.

SMALL GROUP SESSION IDEAS

Opening (10 minutes)

It will be immediately apparent to the group that this second half of Daniel is very different from the first half. Someone may even observe that Daniel's visions read like a page out of Revelation. Be aware that there are many more parallels to passages in Revelation than we have identified in this lesson. If we were to take the time to study each of them in depth, this study guide would go on for many more chapters!

At this point you may want to ask if anyone looked up the term *apocalyptic literature* (see the optional study project at the end of lesson 6). Invite persons who researched this term to explain what they learned. (In case no one else did the exercise, you'll want to come prepared with an explanation of the term.) Take a few moments to discuss this unique type of biblical literature—its form, content, and purpose.

Prayer—Since these chapters of Daniel are closely related to Revelation, begin your opening prayer with words of praise from Revelation 4:8, 11: "'Holy, holy, holy is the Lord God Almighty, who was, and is, and is to come.' . . . 'You are worthy, our Lord and God, to receive glory and honor and power, for you created all things, and by your will they were created and have their being.'" (You could also sing the words of these passages, familiar to many Christians in popular hymns and praise songs.) Then continue by asking God for eyes of faith to see clearly the meaning of the visions in Daniel 7-8.

Share—One of the goals suggested in session 6 was to compliment someone who allowed his or her faith to show. Ask if people followed through on this suggestion, and if so, encourage them to share how it felt to be an encourager. You could also take a moment to think about this question together: *Why don't we encourage people this way more often?*

Focus—Daniel's visions of future kingdoms may seem far removed from our daily work, play, church, and family life. Keep in mind that the ultimate message—not just in Daniel's day but for all time—is that God is firmly in control of *all* the world's events. Group members could also focus on this message by asking questions like these: *"How can I be sure that God is in control today? How can I have faith that God is in control of my life?*

Growing (35-40 minutes)

Read (optional)—Since the vision accounts in Daniel are quite different from the faith stories in Daniel 1-6, you might want to try a different approach for reading the passages (which are also quite long). For example, four group members could read the two chapters for this session in four parts: vision (7:1-14), interpretation (7:15-28), vision (8:1-14), interpretation (8:15-27).

Discuss—Use the following questions to supplement those in the General Discussion section. These questions aim to help bridge the gap from Daniel's beastly visions to the faith challenges surrounding us today.

- Daniel was probably in his late sixties when he had these troubling dreams. Why do you think God waited till Daniel was an older adult before sending these visions? In what ways does age affect our thinking about God's control over our lives?

- God gave Daniel not only visions but also heavenly interpreters to help explain them. How does God "interpret" the Word for us today? Who can help guide us in our understanding of God's will? Do we take full advantage of the help that's available? Why or why not?

- The angel Gabriel told Daniel that the vision of the ram and goat concerned "the time of the end" (8:17). Do Daniel's visions make you more or less anxious about the end of time and God's final judgment? Explain.

- It's clear from Daniel's dreams that God allows certain people and nations to run amok, deceiving and destroying even among God's people. Why would God allow such deception and destruction among the faithful? To what extent do such things teach punishment for disobedience, or even help bring people to faith? Think about and discuss current examples in which God has used hardship and persecution to spread and deepen faith.

Goalsetting (5 minutes)

In the coming week, keep an eye out for "signs of the end" such as those described by Jesus in Matthew 24. Where do you see enemies of God at work? Where do you see wars and rumors of wars? What natural events show that the creation itself has been deeply affected by sin? Be prepared to discuss how a greater awareness of these things can lead to a strengthening of faith.

Closing (10 minutes)

Preparing for Prayer—Read together Revelation 18:1-8 about the fall of Babylon. Take a few moments to think silently about the ways in which we participate in the deception and destruction of our own society. How does Daniel encourage us to live instead? Invite group members also to mention personal concerns and praises.

Prayer—Turn next to Revelation 15:3-4 and read the words of the song there as the opening to your prayer. Continue by asking for the strength and courage to live by faith as we see human kingdoms rise and fall in this world. Invite group members to add other prayer items as well. Then close, if you like, with a familiar song of praise, such as "Great and Mighty Is the Lord Our God" or "Now Blessed Be the Lord Our God."

Group Project (Optional)

In our Scripture for lesson 8, Daniel begins by offering a prayer of confession on behalf of God's exiled people. Some of you may wish to gather prayers of confession from orders of worship, books of prayer, and other prayer resources. You might also like to try writing such a prayer of your own. Be prepared to use one of these at the beginning of your next study session. You could also make copies of prayers for others in the group to use during personal times of devotion.

DANIEL 9:1-11:1

God's Messengers

In a Nutshell

When Daniel offers a prayer of confession for the people of Israel, God immediately sends the angel Gabriel to deliver a response (Dan. 9). Then, a few years later, while Daniel is standing on the bank of the Tigris River, God sends a heavenly "man dressed in linen" to tell him about the future of his people. In both appearances, God's messengers bring Daniel a word of encouragement and strength. The prophet's testimony reminds all people of faith that God not only hears our prayers but also sends angels to work on our behalf.

Best-Sellers: Prayers and Angels

Although there is some prophetic material to consider in these chapters, group members may be pleasantly surprised to find that the main emphases for this lesson are prayer and angels. These two subjects have become very popular in the past couple of decades, even in the secular media. Mountains of books and teaching materials have been produced on prayer—and hopefully these have led to a proportional increase in the amount of time people actually spend praying. For years now we've also seen angels highlighted in all kinds of media; they've even been featured in jewelry items such as "the angel on my shoulder"!

Unfortunately, much of our culture's attention to both prayer and angels has been more sentimental than biblical, more commercially driven than developed from a perceived need to spend more time with God or to learn from the angels' example of serving God obediently and faithfully.

In light of this, consider devoting a significant portion of your opening time together in prayer. You may wish to use Daniel's prayer in 9:4-19 as a guide. Note especially how the prophet names God's attributes as a way of laying claim to God's promises. God "keeps his covenant of love" (9:4). The Lord is a God who is "righteous" (9:7) in judgment as well as "merciful and forgiving" (9:9). "In keeping with all your righteous acts," Daniel says, "turn away your anger and your wrath from Jerusalem, your city, your holy hill" (9:16). In other words, Daniel understands that the Lord is the compassionate, promise-keeping God of Israel (Ex. 34:6-7), who has chosen a people and a place to bear God's holy Name (Dan. 9:19; see Deut. 12:11; 2 Sam. 7:11-16).

Why Pray Now?

Some members of your group might wonder why Daniel would choose this time in his exile to make such an impassioned plea for Jerusalem. It could be, of course, that Daniel often prayed this way. One thing we know is that his faithfulness in prayer was no secret; it even got him thrown into a den of lions at around this same time in his life (Dan. 6:1-16; 9:1-2). Nonetheless it's interesting that this is the first time we read of Daniel the exile praying for the restoration of the holy city.

Daniel himself tells us he was reading from the prophecy of Jeremiah (an important indication that the words of the earlier prophets were already being circulated and regarded as Scripture). From "the word of the LORD given to Jeremiah the prophet" Daniel understood that the exile in Babylon was to last seventy years (Dan. 9:2; Jer. 25:11). Daniel also knew from Jeremiah that God would make Babylon itself desolate after the seventy years had passed (25:12). As the study guide points out, since Belshazzar, the last of the Babylonians, had been dethroned and Darius the Mede was now in power, Daniel may have believed that now was the time for the exiles to begin returning home.

There's an important application in this part of Daniel's story: *Daniel's reading of the Word of God taught him what to pray.* That's a helpful lesson for us, especially if we often feel that we don't know what to pray for. God's Word teaches us how to pray and what to pray for.

A More Important Teaching

Recall that while Daniel was still praying, the angel Gabriel appeared to him with an answer. Daniel knew who it was because he had seen Gabriel before, after receiving the vision of the ram and the goat (Dan. 8:16-17). Well worth noting here is that Gabriel came to *instruct* the prophet (9:22). We often think of angels in terms of protection, comfort, or guidance, but here we see that God's angel was sent to teach.

Daniel had been thinking about the seventy years of Jeremiah's prophecy as an indication that God's people might soon return to Jerusalem, but Gabriel came to speak about a more important deliverance. Deeper than the meaning of the "seventy 'sevens'" and of related historical events was the promise that God's complete deliverance would eventually come (9:24).

Israel's suffering wasn't done yet, and neither is ours. Though Jesus the Messiah, "the Anointed One," has come and has atoned for wickedness (9:24), we as God's people continue to experience suffering as we await the return of Christ, in a way like the exiled Jews suffered as they awaited their return to Jerusalem. We can have perfect confidence that when our "seventy 'sevens'" are fulfilled, Christ will return and free us from our temporary exile in this dark world. Then we will see "an end to sin," and in the new heaven and earth the Lord will "bring in everlasting righteousness" (9:24).

Prelude to the Final Vision
Daniel 10:1-11:1 is actually a prelude to the vision portrayed in chapters 11-12, as we've noted in the study guide. The picture of the messenger dressed in linen and how Daniel interacts with him gives us plenty to think about in this lesson, however, before we begin concentrating on the angel's message in our next lesson.

As the study guide points out, Daniel's reaction to the appearance of this messenger was one of sheer terror. His reaction must have been so strong that the other people with him—who could not see the angel—"fled and hid themselves" (10:7).

Like Gabriel in the earlier vision (9:23), this angel stated that Daniel was "highly esteemed" (10:11). Take a few moments with your group, if possible, to discuss why God would have "highly esteemed" Daniel (see General Discussion question 2). How would it make us feel to hear that said of us? As part of your discussion, consider reflecting on a similar statement to Mary in Luke 1:28. (See also Matt. 25:21, 23.)

As Daniel was soon to learn, the angel who came to instruct him was there also to encourage and strengthen him to receive a powerful message "written in the Book of Truth" (Dan. 10:21). Daniel would need the strength and courage to hear, understand, and remember the great vision of the end that he was about to receive.

GENERAL DISCUSSION

1. *How would you react if someone told you that he or she had had an encounter with an angel? Would you believe that person? Why or why not?*

Pastors are often privileged to hear stories that might not be shared with other people. In the eighteen years in which I've been a pastor in three different congregations, I've lost track of the number of times people have told me about mysterious visitors, comforting dreams and visions, and other mysterious messengers and messages from God.

One such person was a young man dying of cancer. Overnight his spirit changed from one of bitterness and anger to one of peace and even joy. I was amazed to hear of a vision he said he'd received, and he was unswervingly sure of its authenticity.

A married couple once confided to me about their mountaintop highway experience. When they suffered car trouble in a very dangerous location, they were surprised when a man in a pickup quickly pulled up behind them. He knew exactly the kind of help they needed and where to find it. After he drove them back to their car, however, and they wanted to pay him for his help, he was nowhere to be found!

As I mentioned in an earlier lesson, I also had an experience with a vision one night, and I'm confident it was a personal gift from God. It was a message for me alone, it was clearly consistent with God's Word, and I share it only rarely because I don't believe God meant it to be shared—at least not yet.

All of these experiences convince me that people have encounters with angels more often than we tend to expect. Sometimes people can be clearly aware of an angel visit, but much more often they aren't aware—and that's probably as God intends. Just as angels are fighting spiritual battles for the Lord on our behalf while they're out of our sight (Dan. 10:13, 20; Eph. 2:1-5; 6:12; Rev. 12), so they also teach, comfort, guide, and protect us, usually without our being aware of their activity. The author of Hebrews knew this teaching to be true, advising, "Do not forget to entertain strangers, for by so doing some people have entertained angels without knowing it" (Heb. 13:2).

2. What qualities in Daniel led both of his heavenly visitors to describe him as "highly esteemed" (Dan. 9:23; 10:11)? How would you feel if an angel said that to you?

As people begin calling out characteristics that might lead to Daniel's being "highly esteemed," you might want to list them on a chalkboard or newsprint for all to see. After studying more than half of the book of Daniel so far, group members will probably be able to come up with a long list of good qualities associated with the prophet.

Perhaps the item at the top of the list should be *obedience.* From his first days in Babylon, Daniel was determined to obey the Lord's commands. He chose not to eat the king's royal food, and God rewarded him for his obedience. The same was true when Daniel ignored King Darius's decree about worship and prayer. Daniel chose obedience to a higher law. A bit of conversation about our own obedience could develop into a long and fruitful discussion. For example, you might ask group members to reflect together on how well we tend to pay attention to God's Ten Commandments in our day-to-day living.

Another attribute we could associate with Daniel is *truth.* Daniel told the truth even when it put his own life at risk. This topic could spark another lengthy discussion, because truth may be even more at risk in our contemporary society than obedience is. From government officials to corporate reports, from media coverage of current events to information sharing between work associates and friends—not to mention gossip!—we often don't know what we can believe anymore. Fewer and fewer people seem to be committed to simply telling the truth.

Daniel was also *faithful in prayer.* His own practice of prayer stands out in several parts of the book bearing his name, and we can see—especially in chapters 2, 6, and 9— that God heard his prayers and often answered them quickly. Knowing that, why wouldn't we pray too?

Other attributes people might mention are Daniel's wisdom (a gift from God—James 1:5), humility, confidence, respect, contentment, discernment, and more. One word sums them all up: *faith.* Daniel was a man of extraordinary faith.

In response to the question about how we'd feel if an angel told us we were "highly esteemed," I imagine that many of us, if honest, would reply, "You must have the wrong person," or "You've got to be kidding—right?" If we thought we actually deserved such a compliment, then the angel certainly would be speaking to the wrong person. But if it drove us to our knees in humility before God, we might in fact be the kind of person God esteems.

As a footnote to this discussion, you could add that there is, of course, a good kind of pride that we might call *righteous pride*. It's characterized mainly by a deep satisfaction (perhaps like the "pure joy" of James 1:2) that comes from living truly humbly by faith, doing one's best to the glory of God, and daily making oneself available to God—all in God's strength and by God's will, not our own. Feeling good about living faithfully is a gift that God gives—along with all other good things (1:17). But if this good pride mixes with selfishness or becomes boasting, we've crossed over to the side of sin, for which God has no esteem.

3. *In his prayer of confession, Daniel made clear that God always acted in righteousness, even in allowing the chosen people to be exiled (Dan. 9:14). Do we still perceive that God is perfectly just in all things? To what degree do we acknowledge our disobedience and its consequences? Explain.*

As society's respect for authority in general declines, there tends to be a corresponding lack of respect for the authority of God. In the past (say, a hundred years ago) most people who believed in God had little or no doubt about God's sovereign righteousness, trusting that whatever God did or allowed was somehow good. But today many believers question God's will and ways all the time.

Everything Daniel said about God in his prayer is true. God, who is all-powerful, merciful, and active, continues to be righteous and just in all things. Most important for us, God loves this world and its people so much that "he gave his one and only Son" to be its Savior, so that all who believe in him can be justified before God (John 3:16; Rom. 3:22-26). This knowledge, more than anything else, should convince us that God is righteous in all things. If we learn nothing else from Daniel, we should at least understand that the course of humanity—past, present, and future—is firmly in God's grasp. The Lord of heaven and earth continues graciously to work out his promised plan of salvation for humanity.

If we refuse to acknowledge God's good sovereignty over all things, we're also not likely to own up to our own sin and shame. Instead, we'll be tempted to contend that all our actions are the result of genetics, upbringing, environment, or some other factor beyond our control.

The more we think that way, the less we tend to come before God to acknowledge our sin, personally or corporately, as Daniel did. Many churches today, for example, have dropped the prayer of confession from their liturgy because they judge it to be a "downer"—and we certainly don't want anyone to feel bad in worship!

How much greater our appreciation of God's grace becomes when we regularly confess our sins and experience the power of forgiveness! As Jesus taught Simon the Pharisee one day, our gratitude and love for God grow stronger when we realize how grievously we have sinned—and that God forgives us in our repentance even though we don't deserve it (Luke 7:41-47). Even several centuries before Jesus came, the prophet Daniel showed that he understood this truth, knowing that the righteous God is powerful to forgive us and keep his promises.

The bottom line is that we have only ourselves to blame for our sin—and only God to thank for freeing us from it. "If we claim to be without sin, we deceive ourselves. . . . If we confess our sins, [God] is faithful and just and will forgive us our sins and purify us from all unrighteousness" (1 John 1:8-9).

4. *Daniel's prayer was answered as soon as he began praying (Dan. 9:23). Why aren't all prayers answered that quickly? Why might God have us wait longer for the answers to some prayers?*

From our earth-bound perspective, not all prayers seem to get rapid responses. In fact, much of the time it can seem that answers are very slow in coming, and sometimes it seems we may not receive an answer at all.

But we have to admit that our perception is often flawed. God does not fail to answer prayers; we sometimes fail to see the answers. And at those times, we often fail to see that God's answer is actually better than what we prayed for.

Consider Jesus' parable of the persistent neighbor (Luke 11:5-13). This pest goes and knocks on his neighbor's door late at night till finally his neighbor gets up and gives him the bread he needs for his guest (notice that he wasn't asking for himself). Jesus points out that if a grouchy, sleepy, annoyed neighbor will answer such a friend's request, how much more won't God give what is needed to those who ask!

Revelation 8:3-5 gives us a picture of how prayer works. In that passage we read of the prayers of the saints rising to heaven, mingled with incense (for purification), and offered on the golden altar before God's throne. So not only does God hear "the prayers of all the saints" (Rev. 8:3-4), but they are also purified as they go up before the Lord. The apostle Paul explains further that it's the Spirit of God who "helps us in our weakness": "We do not know what we ought to pray for, but the Spirit himself intercedes for us with groans that words cannot express. And he who searches our hearts knows the mind of the Spirit, because the Spirit intercedes for the saints in accordance with God's will. And we know that in all things God works for the good of those who love him, who have been called according to his purpose" (Rom. 8:26-28).

So we know that God hears our prayers, and we know that God answers. Why, then, do the answers sometimes seem slow in coming?

This observation may simply be part of the answer itself. It may be that the time isn't right for the answer we want; it may be that other people or situations have to change in some way before we can have the answer we're seeking— and our requests, of course, must be within God's will (John 15:7-8, 16). It may be that God is saying not now or wait or maybe even no to our request. Parents know that they sometimes have to say no when their children believe that the parents can't possibly know what's best for them. God sometimes has to treat us in much the same way. Other times, as we learn from Psalm 66, the Lord may reject our prayer because we haven't fully confessed our sins. In other words, if we're holding back our repentance because of some "cherished sin" (Ps. 66:18), how can we expect God to listen and answer?

5. *What does the appearance of the "man dressed in linen" tell us about this visitor to Daniel?*

As noted in the lesson, the appearance of Daniel's visitor is similar to the description of Jesus given by John in Revelation 1:13-16. But that doesn't mean this visitor was the Lord in a pre-incarnation appearance, as some interpreters have suggested; it clarifies only that Jesus perfectly fulfilled the royal and priestly roles represented by this visitor's appearance and clothing.

The linen is a priestly symbol (see Lev. 6:10 and many other passages), and the golden belt is a sign of royalty and authority (Daniel himself received a chain of gold shortly before Belshazzar's death—Dan. 5:29). The body like chrysolite may refer to a radiant or semi-transparent quality (note also that chrysolite, also known as olivine, is a hard, yellow-green silicate of magnesium and iron). The face like lightning and the eyes like flaming torches are reminiscent of features Ezekiel saw when he also had a vision of heavenly beings (Ezek. 1:13). The arms and legs of burnished bronze also recall a similar description by Ezekiel (1:7), and the voice with a sound like a multitude echoes Isaiah 13:4, where the sound of a great multitude signified that a great army was being assembled for war.

Priestly, with the authority of royalty, and prepared for war—Daniel's visitor must have been a sight to behold!

6. *The messenger explains that he was delayed twenty-one days, the same amount of time Daniel says he was in mourning (Dan. 10:2, 13). Do you think our experiences and even our emotions can be affected by unseen spiritual beings? Explain.*

Our experiences and emotions may well be affected by other beings, though we can't be sure how much or how often. One thing we know for certain is that the fallen angel Satan is looking for ways to tempt and destroy us all the time (1 Pet. 5:8-9).

Consider also the humorous story of Balaam and his donkey in Numbers 22. Balaam couldn't see there was an angel blocking his path; only the donkey could, and the creature wisely refused to go a step farther. When the donkey finally told Balaam why it had stopped, that certainly changed Balaam's course of action, affecting his emotions as well.

Who knows how often we've been confronted by an angel without being aware of it? When our spirits are suddenly lifted, it may be that an angel has done something for us that we don't even know about. When our path takes a sudden new direction, perhaps an unseen angel is directing our way or protecting us from some kind of harm. Without going into too much speculation about the affect of either angels or demons on our everyday lives, we can be assured that God is always in control and that multitudes of heaven's angels are assigned to protecting and guiding God's people in line with God's will (2 Kings 6:15-17; Ps. 34:7; Matt. 18:10; 26:53; Luke 2:9-14; 22:43; Acts 5:19-20; 12:6-10). For a helpful book on the Bible's teachings about angels, see the study project on angels suggested at the end of this lesson.

SMALL GROUP SESSION IDEAS

Opening (10 minutes)

Many people have stories to tell about unusual visitors, mysterious helpers, or even messengers who speak through their dreams. Without going too far into tabloid territory ("An angel told me to play the lottery!"), encourage group members to share some of their own accounts. Also ask everyone to keep this question in mind: *If God were going to send you angelic visitors, when would God send them, and why?*

Prayer—The optional group project at the end of session 7 invited people to write prayers of confession. If any group members did so, invite them to begin this opening prayer time by sharing what they've prepared. Or you could read Psalm 51 together and spend some time in silence as people bring their own private confessions to God.

Share—Take a few minutes to talk about the experience of confession. *How does it make you feel when you've confessed your sins? Are you tempted to make excuses for your behavior, or are you willing to accept responsibility? Do you ever wish you could share your confession with another person, as people do in some faith traditions?* During this discussion, be careful not to pry into the particulars of anyone's confession.

Focus—This lesson focuses on confession, God's response to prayer, and the heavenly beings God sends to convey messages and carry out God's plans. Consider this question as you move through this session: *If God sent Gabriel to speak to you, what message do you think the angel would bring?*

Growing (35-40 minutes)
Read—Since our Scriptures for this lesson are unfamiliar to many people, you may want to ask whether everyone has read them in advance. If not, take the time to read them aloud together.

Discuss—Consider using these questions in addition to those in the General Discussion section.

- What's the relationship between humility, self-esteem, and godly esteem? Do you think it's biblical to encourage everyone to have high self-esteem all the time? Explain.

- How often do we include our nation (or even the church) in our personal prayers? What difference might it make if more believers made this a regular practice?

- Gabriel's message was not a very positive one, filled with wars and desolations. Would you want to know the future, even if it contained bad news? Explain.

- How do modern media images of angels compare with what we find in our Scriptures for this lesson? Why do you think the modern imagery developed the way it did?

Goalsetting (5 minutes)

Keep an eye out for evidence of angels during the coming week. If you can, bring along to the next session some examples of modern portrayals of angels. Do the portrayals honor these special beings? Do they accurately portray angels' roles in protecting and guiding God's people?

Closing (10 minutes)

Preparing for Prayer—This session began with an emphasis on confession. Consider closing with an emphasis on God's assurance of forgiveness. Read Psalm 103 together, and think about how these words apply to the Scriptures for this session. Invite group members also to mention personal concerns and praises they'd like to bring before the Lord.

Prayer—Thank God for hearing our confessions, and for preparing an answer to our prayers as soon as we begin to pray. Ask for humility and for the grace to believe that even now there are heavenly beings all around us. Also invite people to join in with prayer concerns that have been raised.

Group Study Project (Optional)

The final two chapters of Daniel concentrate mainly on the period of history from Daniel's time until the second century B.C. persecutions under Antiochus IV Epiphanes. If group members haven't already located or created a time line of that period (see group project at the end of lesson 1), perhaps they'd like to do so now. They can find help in a good Bible dictionary or handbook, a commentary on Daniel, or on the Internet. Then they could use their research as a visual aid during the final session of this study.

Group Study Project (Optional)

If you'd like to learn more about angels, we recommend *In the Company of Angels: What the Bible Teaches, What You Need to Know* by Andrew Bandstra (CRC Publications, 1995). A leader's guide for group study is also available. Call 1-800-333-8300 or visit *www.FaithAliveResources.org* for more information.

DANIEL 11:2-12:13

Salvation Will Come

In a Nutshell
Daniel now receives a vision that describes the next two and a half centuries of Middle Eastern history. As we listen with Daniel, we realize that the vision describes our future too. In every age the people of God can have faith that the author of history is firmly in control of its future. The angel's closing words to Daniel apply to all who trust in the Lord: "At the end of the days you will rise to receive your allotted inheritance" (Dan. 12:13).

Last Things First
Congratulations! You've made it to the end of this study (almost)! Make sure you let the rest of your group know they deserve congratulations too. The last several chapters of Daniel can be hard going. I hope your group agrees that this study has been worth the effort.

Assure group members that they do not have to learn all the names, dates, and places that correspond with Daniel's final vision (although it never hurts us to learn about important events in history). What's most important is to understand that the prophecies in this vision—at least to the point where the scene shifts to the end of time (at Dan. 11:40)—have been fulfilled. The reason this is so important is that the fulfillment of these prophecies gives us every reason to believe that the remaining prophecies about the end will also be fulfilled, especially this one: "Multitudes who sleep in the dust of the earth will awake: some to everlasting life, others to shame and everlasting contempt. Those who are wise will shine like the brightness of the heavens, and those who lead many to righteousness, like the stars for ever and ever" (12:2-3).

Life in the Middle

One reason that "the Beautiful Land" (11:16, 41), Palestine, figures prominently in the vision and in the history of battles between the Seleucids of Syria and the Ptolemies of Egypt is that it lies squarely between these two regions. It was naturally often a battleground as power shifted from north to south and back again.

As described in the study guide, the many rulers in that period of history, in all of their intermarrying, truce making, treaty breaking, backstabbing, and other nefarious behavior, led up to the rise to power of Antiochus IV Epiphanes. And as we noted in lesson 7, this "little horn" of Daniel 8 was a cruel oppressor of the Jews, and his reign of oppression can be seen as a type of the tribulation that will come at the end of time (see also 7:8, 20-22).

Type Casting

If the concept of types in the Bible is new or unfamiliar to some members of your group, a brief explanation of type casting may help people better understand why Daniel spends so much time on Antiochus IV—an otherwise insignificant ruler, as far as world history is concerned.

A biblical type is an illustration of something or someone yet to come, an event or person that points to the fulfillment of a great promise or prophecy in God's plan to redeem humanity and this world. In some ways a type can be understood as a kind of living prophecy that may continue for many years. The type is *not* the perfect or complete representation of what it points to; it is only similar in some ways, giving observers a general idea of what they are looking for in the actual fulfillment.

For example, Moses, who led the Israelites on their exodus from Egypt to the promised land, was a type of the Savior. He was instrumental in setting his people free, acting as their intermediary with God, and taking them on a journey that demanded their trust and obedience. The people of Israel themselves were a type of the church of the New Testament, which extends into the present day as we journey through life on our way to God's eternal promised land, the new heaven and new earth (Rev. 21-22).

Worship in the tabernacle and temple of the Old Testament became a type of the worship in the church of the New Testament. Sacrifices and rituals performed by the priests—who were a type of our eternal High Priest, Jesus—were a type of the gifts of praise and gratitude we now offer in worship. Many other examples of types occurring in the Old Testament are fulfilled in the New Testament, especially in connection with Jesus, whose life, death, and resurrection are the pivot point of world history.

Antiochus IV Epiphanes didn't know it, but he represented several types of a different kind: he was a type of many antichrists who would oppress the people of God in years to come (Mark 13:5-23; 2 Thess. 2:3-4; 1 John 2:18); he was a type for the final antichrist of Revelation (see Rev. 13; 19:19-21); and his three and a half years of oppression were a type of the final great tribulation mentioned in Revelation 7:14. What's more, all of these antichrists point ultimately to the great enemy, Satan, who also will eventually be overthrown and sentenced to everlasting punishment when the Lord returns to judge the living and dead (Dan. 7:9-14; Rev. 20:10-21:5).

Intense Speculation

Many people have grown wealthy by capitalizing on the uncertainty in the remainder of Daniel's prophecy. With a bit of creativity here and a nod to the book of Revelation there, they concoct elaborate scenarios for the future that sound plausible to many eager listeners. Where the Bible makes no attempt to identify specific people, times, or places, such clever writers have filled in details from their own imaginations, claiming to have "solved" a mystery that the Bible never intended to be mysterious.

The purpose of apocalyptic texts like these in Daniel and like several others in Revelation is first and foremost to provide comfort and assurance to the people of God in every generation. Yes, there may be terrible things happening; yes, there are wars in heaven and on earth; yes, the faithful will be tempted to abandon the ways of God; and yes, there will be a "time of distress such as has not happened from the beginning of nations" (Dan. 12:1). But the purpose of such prophecies is not to encourage us to figure it all out so that we might know the time of the end, but rather to *be prepared at any time* for the coming of the end.

Jesus himself said, "No one knows about that day or hour, not even the angels in heaven, nor the Son, but only the Father." (Matt. 24:36). Far too much of the writing that's been done about passages like this one in Daniel are focused on trying to figure out when the end is going to come. Jesus makes clear, though, that he will return without warning and that our challenge is to be prepared at all times.

Salvation Will Come

The final verses of Daniel contain a wonderful surprise for any-one who may never have read to the end of the book before. There we unexpectedly find what is probably the most com-plete statement in the Old Testament about the resurrection of the dead: "Multitudes who sleep in the dust of the earth will awake: some to everlasting life, others to shame and everlasting contempt" (Dan. 12:2). This statement requires no creative imagination; the angel tells us exactly what it means: "Those who are wise will shine like the brightness of the heavens, and those who lead many to righteousness, like the stars for ever and ever" (12:3).

Who are these wise people? Having worked our way to the end of this book of prophecy, wouldn't we have to say that they're the people who, like Daniel, live by faith in obedience to the one true God? Just as we've seen the prophet guided by faith in God in every situation, so we are being taught that we too can always trust in God.

Daniel's statement merely prepares us for the New Testa-ment's fuller explanation of salvation by faith in Jesus alone, but even if we never turned to the New Testament, we would see from Daniel's example that there is a right way for exiles to live. Should we conform to the standards of the world in which we find ourselves for a time? Or should we continue to live by faith in God until the Lord brings us home?

Daniel teaches us that there is only one correct answer to that question: *People who want to live with God live by faith.*

GENERAL DISCUSSION

1. *What is the relationship between prophecy and faith? The prophecies in Daniel 11 and 12 cover the rise and fall of several kingdoms over hundreds of years. Are these prophecies as effective in encouraging people to remain faithful as the stories in the first half of Daniel are? How do prophecies affect our faith differently than stories do?*

   In some ways, prophecies may be even more useful than stories in encouraging people to live by faith. The sad truth of living in a sin-affected world is that for every Daniel who has been spared from death at the teeth of hungry lions, countless other faithful Christians have been devoured. This doesn't mean that their faith was foolish or that God loved them less than Daniel. It's just that their stories may not do as much as a Daniel story does to inspire faith.

With the prophecies of the Bible, we have an opportunity to see God's Word being fulfilled as time goes on. We don't have to wonder whether God's Word is trustworthy. Prophecies, along with their fulfillment, assure us that faith in the Lord is not in vain.

Deuteronomy 18:22 tells us how to test prophets and their prophecies: "If what a prophet proclaims in the name of the LORD does not take place or come true, that is a message the LORD has not spoken." Thus we find the relationship between prophecy and faith in both the prophecy and its fulfillment. When we read a prophetic word, we believe by faith that what it says will come to pass. When it does come to pass, our faith is confirmed. As a result, we continue to believe biblical prophecies that await fulfillment, having every reason to trust that God will fulfill them. Another important thing to know about prophecy is that it doesn't always involve predicting something about the future. Prophecy is first of all a word of the Lord to God's people in their particular time and setting. So any preaching of the Word of God is prophecy, and that sometimes includes warnings and revelations (apocalypses) about things to come.

For many people, a good story will always do more to inspire faithfulness than a prophecy and its fulfillment. There's no denying the power of personal testimony, which is what the first half of Daniel is all about. But neither is there any denying the power of prophecy such as we find in the second half of Daniel—whether it's fulfilled, still awaiting fulfillment, or awaiting further fulfillment. How marvelous that the book of Daniel includes something to encourage everyone's faith!

2. *Most of the prophecies in Daniel 11 pointed to a specific time— the years between the end of Israel's captivity and the desecration of the rebuilt temple in Jerusalem in 168-167 B.C.—but they also have a message for our time. What lessons for today can we find in these passages?*

There's hardly a passage in God's Word that can't teach us something for today. In the opening parts of Daniel's final vision, just a few of the messages that can apply to us today include the fleeting nature of earthly power (Dan. 11:4), the powerlessness of idols (11:8), and the inevitable fate of the proud and insolent (11:18-19). From there, we move on to the folly of basing our security on anything material or earthly (11:24), the often-divided nature of evil (11:27), and the corruption of worship at the hands of the wicked

101

(11:31). That makes for six hefty sermon topics in just a few paragraphs of Scripture!

Daniel's vision also carries the message that in many respects the prophecies here have been fulfilled. From shifts in political allegiance to palace intrigue to the desecration of the temple, God saw it all coming. And now we who read the words of Daniel many years later can see that, most important, the Lord was firmly in control of all these events.

In addition, some parts of Daniel's prophecy still await fulfillment or further fulfillment. So these words from the Lord teach us to wait in hope for the time of the end—obediently, patiently, and with our faith intact.

If we were to dismiss Daniel's vision as being only for a specific time or place, we'd also have to discard many other prophecies in the Old Testament. Even though many point us specifically toward Jesus, in whom they are completely fulfilled, many others are more concerned with immediate or repeating historical situations. In a similar way, many of the New Testament letters addressed particular concerns of local congregations—and yet all of those passages also contain a message for today.

This is the miracle of the Bible—that the words spoken and recorded so many years ago can still guide God's people today. It truly is a living Word: "Sharper than any double-edged sword, it penetrates even to dividing soul and spirit, joints and marrow; it judges the thoughts and attitudes of the heart" (Heb. 4:12). Inspired by God, "all Scripture . . . is useful for teaching, rebuking, correcting and training in righteousness" (2 Tim. 3:16).

3. *The angel said that "the people who know their God will firmly resist" false teachers, tyrants, and other corrupting influences (Dan. 11:32). What are some ways in which people have sold out their faith today? What effect has this had on worship? With such strong cultural forces arrayed against us, how can believers remain faithful to God?*

When we read all of Daniel 11:32 again within its context, we can see that the ruler who was desecrating worship deceived some of God's people "with flattery." There may well be no force more antithetical to worship than the temptation to make it about ourselves or appealing to ourselves.

Worship is supposed to be about God. God enjoys our company and wants to bring blessing into our lives, but if we begin to turn inward, shutting God out of our worship, we end up substituting a fleeting, emotional caricature of worship for the real thing. Worship that is about us cannot begin to offer the abundant, lasting benefits God desires to give us through worship.

People have "sold out" their faith in many ways, corrupting their worship in the process. Many people today have also decided that earthly wealth is more important than spiritual wealth. They've chosen personal comfort ahead of serving others. People also have decided to use their time and talents selfishly, rather than offering them for God to use.

The effect of all this on worship is startling and devastating. But before identifying specific consequences, we need to understand that just because something in worship is new or different, it's not necessarily corrupt. There's a great deal about contemporary worship, for example, that is actually truer to the direction of Scripture than much of what many of us know as traditional worship. Here are some simple test questions: *Does the worship element or activity under discussion draw our attention to God or to a person (or people)? Does it make us more aware of God or more aware of ourselves?* Anything that draws our attention away from what God is doing in worship should probably be avoided.

In what ways might we be focusing on ourselves and our desires rather than on God in our worship? I can think of a few examples, and your group members can probably think of several others. While some of these may sound to you like personal preferences, please consider and pray about them. Ultimately our goal together as God's people is to bring glory to God in all we do, especially when we gather for worship. That calls for listening to each other and making "every effort to keep the unity of the Spirit through the bond of peace" (Eph. 4:3).

One example I've noticed is that some of what is called contemporary Christian music suffers from a strong secular bias. I'm talking about songs in which you can substitute the word "baby" for "Jesus" and have it make just as much sense. To me, that's a clue that the theology or perhaps even the intent of the song may be suspect. On the other hand, there are also many new worship songs today that are straight from Scripture—and they're wonderful! Also excellent and beautiful are many songs that mine deep biblical truths in fresh ways—and often with a variety of musical styles. The watchword in worship music should be that "whatever is true . . . noble . . . right . . . excellent or praiseworthy—think about such things," for "every good and perfect gift" is from God and can be used to glorify God (Phil. 4:8; James 1:17).

Dress is another area that requires careful attention. Attire for worship has certainly changed in the past few decades. Wearing a tie or skirt certainly isn't holier than wearing an open-collared shirt or slacks. But bared shoulders or midriffs—not to mention a great deal of male and female summer attire—can draw attention to the person and away from God. That's where we cross the line of what is and is not appropriate.

It's saddening also that many churches have dropped the prayer of confession because they choose to avoid anything in worship that might cause someone to feel guilt or shame. Another sign of weakening in this area is that many churches give little or no attention to the Ten Commandments, and very few include a weekly reading of the Law to remind worshipers of God's guidelines for grateful living. These elements, possibly more than any other, make us aware of how much we need God and God's grace in our lives (Heidelberg Catechism, Q&A 115).

This discussion could go on and on, but what we do not want to forget is the way in which believers can stand firm: *Test everything against God's Word.* The Bible reveals how God desires to be worshiped, and if we can't find scriptural support for something in our worship, we may want to think again about who we're actually worshiping.

4. *Daniel 12:1 reminds us again that the battle against evil is being fought not only here on earth but also between good and fallen angels (see 10:13, 20-11:1). In what ways, if any, does this affect your thinking about angels? How do you think guardian angels protect us?*

Angels are rarely depicted as warriors in the media. As we've noted earlier in this study, popular renditions of angels tend to be, well, angelic. They're often either cute little cherubs, members of a harp-playing choir, or winged versions of recently deceased human beings. (*Note:* It may be necessary to make clear that human beings do *not* become angels when they pass away from this life on earth. Angels are an altogether different order of being. It appears that while they do protect us and bring God's messages to us, they do not understand everything about God's salvation of human beings—see 1 Pet. 1:12.)

What the Bible often reveals to us when it speaks of angels are that they are fierce warriors, terrifying in appearance—anything but cute. From Daniel's vision we learn that angels are fighting battles on our behalf; these angels protect God's people by battling other (fallen) angels who serve the powers of evil (Dan. 10:13, 20-11:1; 12:1).

The concept of a personal guardian angel comes from two places in the Bible: Psalm 34:7 says, "The angel of the LORD encamps around those who fear him, and he delivers them." We might dismiss this as mere poetry if we didn't also have this word from Jesus: "See that you do not look down on one of these little ones. For I tell you that their angels in heaven always see the face of my Father in heaven" (Matt. 18:10).

You may want to spend some time discussing how angels protect us. Do they steer cars out of harm's way (a popular notion)? Perhaps they do—sometimes. But since their title means "messenger," perhaps their best protection comes from reminding us to believe and obey God's Word. (If you or any other group members would like to study more about angels, see the group study project on angels at the end of lesson 8.)

5. *In Daniel 12:2, 13 we find (somewhat as a surprise) references about the resurrection of the dead. How do you think Daniel's readers might have reacted to this idea? How strongly is this belief still held today? What kind of evidence shows that people believe in the resurrection to everlasting life?*

It's hard to imagine how Daniel's original readers might have reacted to this prophecy about an afterlife. Up to the time of Daniel, the general belief about an afterlife was that people's souls or spirits went to Sheol, the place of the dead, which was generally thought to be beneath the earth (see Job 24:19; Isa. 38:10). There is little indication in the Old Testament of any widespread hope of joining God for eternity. The emphasis was on experiencing God's blessings in this life. (But see also Job 19:25-27; Ps. 16:9-11.)

Because of this, Daniel's readers may have thought that the promise of "everlasting life" (Dan. 12:2) meant they would return to more of this life. For some, that might have been good news, but it may not have sounded so good to people who faced a lot of struggle in this life. The possibility of returning to shame and everlasting contempt must also have seemed daunting. Anyone who experienced the shadow of contempt in the Jewish community—cut off from acceptance and fellowship even because of chronic illness, childlessness, or poverty, for example—knew that that was a terrible way to live. Who, if they weren't accepted among God's people in this life, would want to return to an existence like that—or far worse?

From our perspective, knowing that the angel was talking about a new kind of life, it may be hard to imagine that anyone wouldn't embrace this promise. And yet in our society, with so much emphasis on worldly wealth and personal comfort—even within the church—some people seem to believe this life is all there is. Many of us can think of situations in which we see more evidence of storing up "treasures on earth" than of storing up "treasures in heaven" (Matt. 6:19-20).

Many other examples, though, show that people believe in the resurrection to everlasting life. At the foundation of their life is faith in the eternal, sovereign Lord. In the same way that faith set Daniel apart as an extraordinary servant of God, so faith today is our best evidence that someone believes God's promises. Where we find faith, we are almost certain to find someone who not only believes but also lives in hope and shows love for God, for all people, and for God's creation, trusting that God's promises are true. (For some ideas about practicing faith by living in hope and showing God's love, see the group project suggested at the end of this lesson.)

SMALL GROUP SESSION IDEAS

Opening (10 minutes)

Since this is the last session of this study, invite people to take a few moments to discuss what they've learned from their study of Daniel. Have there been any surprises? Have they found Daniel to be helpful in addressing some of the faith challenges they face each day?

Prayer—As a prayer of gratitude for God's gift of the book of Daniel, consider beginning your prayer time by reading Psalm 16 (verse 8 could almost be a summary statement of Daniel's entire life). Ask the Holy Spirit for wisdom to understand God's meaning for us in Daniel's final vision, in which even the cast of characters can be confusing.

Share—Ask if anyone has found or prepared a time line that depicts the series of kings and kingdoms following the Babylonian Empire. (See the study project suggestion at the end of session 8.) If no one has, you may want to make a list of these on a board or newsprint during this session.

Focus—Daniel's final vision focuses on God's control: over all of human history, and over the everlasting life we'll enjoy when earthly history is complete. Try keeping this question in mind throughout this session: *As I study Daniel's prophecies about the continuing course of life in this world and the promise of the life to come, how is my faith affected?*

Growing (35-40 minutes)

Read—The Scriptures for this lesson are long passages with a large cast of characters. So it may be helpful to read a paragraph at a time, pausing in between to identify various parallels with Middle Eastern history a few centuries before Christ (much of this is covered in the study guide). Be aware that at Daniel 11:40 the prophecy shifts to portray events at the end of time.

Discuss—The following questions are designed to help everyone respond to the lesson material in a personal way as the group works through the questions for General Discussion.

- If an angel offered to tell you the general course of world history for the next few hundred years, would you want to know it? Why or why not? How could you use that knowledge to encourage people now or in the future to be faithful to God?

- Why do you think God allowed the Jews to be persecuted by Antiochus IV Epiphanes? What effect does persecution have on faith? (Consider Dan. 11:35.) Take a few moments to discuss some situations today in which believers are suffering under persecution.

- With the great sweep of history under God's control and with heavenly angels doing battle on our behalf, what prevents us from being mere pawns in some celestial game of chess?

- What lasting impression does Daniel leave on you? Does Daniel's example inspire you to live a more faith-filled life? Explain.

Goalsetting (5 minutes)

Encourage everyone to accept the challenge of living in the world the way Daniel lived in Babylon. Even though much was foreign and even hostile toward his faith, he lived in line with God's Word. Take a few moments to list some of the ways our society works against us when we make a decision to live by faith. Commit together to resist temptations and to be faithful, in God's strength.

Closing (10 minutes)

Preparing for Prayer—Mention some things you've learned from this study of Daniel, and be prepared to thank God for them specifically. Encourage everyone also to think of a one-word description of the thing they need most if they're going to keep living by faith. If everyone is willing, go around the group and share these one-word prayer requests. Invite everyone also to share other concerns and praises.

Prayer—Read Psalm 16 (again) to begin your closing prayer. Thank God for all you've learned together while studying the life and prophecy of Daniel. Include any other prayer requests that have been shared. Then close, if you like, with a song of hope and faith such as "Lord of All Hopefulness" or "Rejoice, O Pure in Heart."

Group Project (Optional)

Some or all of your group members may be interested in a cause that looks ahead in faith, hope, and love. When God's kingdom comes in all its fullness, we will live with God; the earth will be restored; wars will cease; and pain, persecution, and suffering will be no more. The picture of resurrection to "everlasting life" in Daniel 12:2 points us to the great hope we have of living in God's presence forever. It also reminds us of ways we can serve in God's power to help bring the beginnings of peace and righteousness (justice) into our world today. For ideas and help in getting started on a project by which you can express your hope in Christ, check with health, welfare, political action, denominational, and environmental agencies.

For example, you could participate in a local immunization clinic, a blood drive, or a food program. Or you could help clean up a roadway, waterway, or disaster site. Or you could work toward human rights, legal justice, AIDS relief, community safety, literacy and basic skills education, biblical literacy, acceptance and education of mentally impaired persons, responsible medical research, preservation of wildlife, proper use of land, cleaner air and water—whatever you can think of. Every area of our lives and of this world is under Christ's authority, and he calls us to seek God's kingdom and righteousness even as we live in this world (Deut. 20:19-20; 22:6-7; Ps. 24:1-2; Matt. 6:33; Luke 12:31; Eph. 1:9-10; Rev. 22:1-2).

Evaluation

Background

Size of group:
- ☐ fewer than 5 persons
- ☐ 5-10
- ☐ 10-15
- ☐ more than 15

Age of participants:
- ☐ 20-30
- ☐ 31-45
- ☐ 46-60
- ☐ 61-75 or above

Length of group sessions:
- ☐ under 60 minutes
- ☐ 60-75 minutes
- ☐ 75-90 minutes
- ☐ 90-120 minutes or more

Please check items that describe you:
- ☐ male
- ☐ female
- ☐ ordained or professional church staff person
- ☐ elder or deacon
- ☐ professional teacher
- ☐ church school or catechism teacher (three or more years' experience)
- ☐ trained small group leader

Study Guide and Group Process

Please check items that describe the material in the study guide:
- ☐ varied
- ☐ monotonous
- ☐ creative
- ☐ dull
- ☐ clear
- ☐ unclear
- ☐ interesting to participants
- ☐ uninteresting to participants
- ☐ too much
- ☐ too little
- ☐ helpful, stimulating
- ☐ not helpful or stimulating
- ☐ overly complex, long
- ☐ appropriate level of difficulty

Please check items that describe the group sessions:
- ☐ lively
- ☐ dull
- ☐ dominated by leader
- ☐ involved most participants
- ☐ relevant to lives of participants
- ☐ irrelevant to lives of participants
- ☐ worthwhile
- ☐ not worthwhile

In general I would rate this material as
- ☐ excellent
- ☐ very good
- ☐ good
- ☐ fair
- ☐ poor

Leader's Guide and Group Process

Please check items that describe the material provided in the leader's guide:
- ☐ helpful, stimulating
- ☐ not helpful or stimulating
- ☐ overly complex, long
- ☐ appropriate level of difficulty
- ☐ clear
- ☐ unclear

The Bible study in general was true to the Reformed/Presbyterian tradition.
- ☐ agree
- ☐ disagree
- ☐ not sure

Please check the procedures that worked best for you:
- ☐ reading of Scripture
- ☐ reading of study-guide notes
- ☐ small group discussions
- ☐ whole-group discussions
- ☐ general-discussion questions
- ☐ focus questions
- ☐ process questions
- ☐ goalsetting
- ☐ group projects
- ☐ other (please write in)

Additional comments on any aspect of this Bible study:

Name (optional): _____
_____
_____
Church: _____
_____
_____
City/State/Province: _____
_____
_____

Please send completed form to

Word Alive / Daniel
Faith Alive Christian Resources
2850 Kalamazoo Ave. SE
Grand Rapids, MI 49560

Thank you!